IN SEARCH OF IRISH SAINTS

In Search of Irish Saints

THE PEREGRINATIO PRO CHRISTO

RÓISÍN NÍ MHEARA

FOUR COURTS PRESS

This book was typeset
in 10.5 on 12.5 Ehrhardt for
FOUR COURTS PRESS
Kill Lane, Blackrock, Co. Dublin

and in the United States of America
FOUR COURTS PRESS
c/o International Specialized Book Services
5804 NE Hassalo St, Portland, OR 97213

ISBN 1–85182–138–4

A catalogue record for this book is available from the British Library.

Printed in Ireland by Betaprint, Dublin

CONTENTS

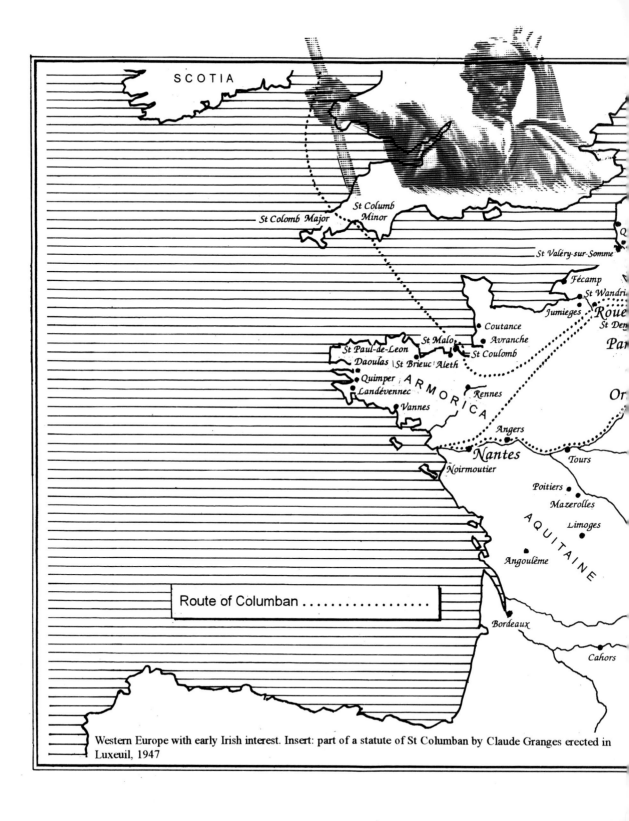

SCOTIA

St Colomb Major
St Columb Minor

St Valéry-sur-Somme

Fécamp
St Wandri
Jumieges
Roue
St Den
Coutance
Avranche
St Malo
St Paul-de-Leon
St Coulomb
Daoulas St Brieuc Aleth
Par
Quimper
ARMORICA
Landévennec
Rennes
Or
Vannes

Angers
Nantes
Tours
Noirmoutier
Poitiers
Mazerolles
Limoges
A
Q
U
I
T
A
I
N
E
Angoulême

Route of Columban . . . .

Bordeaux

Cahors

Western Europe with early Irish interest. Insert: part of a statute of St Columban by Claude Granges erected in Luxeuil, 1947

ACKNOWLEDGEMENTS

I am deeply appreciative of assistance received from a wide range of institutions. Apart from permission given to reproduce material from their libraries and archives – the evidence of which graces these pages – their courtesy often extended to imparting invaluable information. If space does not allow all to be named, special thanks must go to the Benedictine abbey Notre-Dame-de-Jouarre (archivist, Sr. Telchilde de Montessus; the municipal library of Laon (librarian, Mme S. Martinet); the Landesamt für Denkmalpflege, Mainz (Dr Günther Stenzl); the dean of the collegiate church, Fosses-la-Ville, M. l'Abbé Pol Bero; M. le Pasteur Auguste Koch, St Thomas', Strasbourg; and the church authorities of St Wendel, Saarland. Equally obliging were guardians and secretaries of private societies such as the Association Internationale des Amis de Saint Colomban, Luxeuil; Les Amis de Saint-Florent Niederhaslach, Alsace; the Cercle d'Études Archéologiques et Historiques du Pays de Lagny-sur-Marne; the Centre Culturel de Plestin-les-Grèves, Brittany; and the Historischer Verein, Ettenheim. Permission was also gratefully received for the reproduction of manuscripts in the care of the Bibliothèque Nationale de Paris, the Bibliothèque Municipale of Péronne and the Schottenstift-bibliothek in Vienna; Prof R. Thirion-Ninane graciously permitted the publication of one of her diagrams of the sarcophagus of Chrodoara d'Amay – a discovery made by her husband in 1977.

Of the photographic illustrations listed below special mention must be made of the editor of the Munich publishing firm Knaur, Herr Franz Mehling, for his generosity in providing material, as also of Mr A.A. Van der Heyden (Naarden, Holland), M. Ph. Kahn (Luxeuil), M. A. Bernard (St-Benoît), and Herr H.W. Luther (St Wendel), whose personal commitment to this project far exceeded their photographic work.

To the town mayor of Luxeuil-Les-Bains, M. Bernard Hagemann, and to local historians Herr Bernhard Uttenweiler (Ettenheim), M. Ernst Eschbach (Molsheim), M. Jean Boutouiller (Plestin-les-Grèves, Brittany), as well as to my son, Dr Roderich Jakobi (Vienna), thanks are equally due for their kind co-operation.

These acknowledgements would not be complete without saluting the memory of the Irish primate Cardinal Tomás Ó Fiaich, scholar and pioneer in the field of research here under scrutiny. It was his fervent wish that this guidebook should appear and but for his untimely death in 1990 he would have been its main contributor.

Finally, I wish to record my gratitude to the publishers for the great care and efficiency shown in preparing this book. *Coir seolta acu leis!*

PHOTOGRAPHIC CREDITS

Black and White Illustrations A. Bernard 15, 16, 17, 18, 19; P. Bero 64; v. Birkenbach 86; J. Boutouiller 26, 27; R. Demont 62; E. Eschback 105; Ettenheimer Bote, Red. 112; R. Jakobi 29, 34, 35, 38, 103, 104, 105, 106, 109, 115, 116, 120, 121, 122; Ph. Kahn 39, 42, 43, 44; Keller, Eds. 123; J. Laubignat 20; H.W. Luther 84; R. Matt 119; F. Mehling 24, 25, 28, 30, 32, 33; R. Muré 108; S. Pfefferle 113; Pretzfeld, Pfarrarchiv 85; K. Reindl 88; Rheinmünster BMA 96; Säckingen, Pfarrarchiv 118; S.A.E.P.: Ingersheim 42; Simon, Eds. 81, 82; G. Stanzl 89, 90; Stollenhofen G-Amt 97; G. Straeter 89; R. Thirion-Ninane 71; B. Uttenweiler 109, 111; A.A. Van der Heyden 23, 45, 58, 59, 60, 63, 65, 66, 68, 69, 70, 71, 72, 74, 75, 76, 77, 78; S. Ware 36; Zodiaque, Eds. 51, 52.

Coloured Plates A. Bernard 9; P. Bero 14; J. Boutouiller 13; C.D.D.P. Melun 3; M-C Fockedey 11, 12; Hansi, Eds. 24; R. Jakobi 1, 6, 10; Ph. Kahn. 19, 20; Keller, Eds. 8; H.W. Luther 7, 15, 21, 23; M. Oehler 4; S. Pfefferle 2, 20; A.A. Van der Heyden 5; S. Ware 16, 17, 18.

Maps and diagrams by the author.

INTRODUCTION

Europe lay in darkness when Ireland enjoyed her Golden Age. Ireland erupted, sending a shower of light down over the scorched earth beyond the sea. Perhaps Ireland just had to overflow.

This book does not aim to give an exhaustive account of the Early Irish mission, which abounds in obscurities and contradictions. It is impossible to trace or ever hope to count the multitude of sandaled feet swarming out into the chaos of post-Roman Europe. Indeed, many of those sandaled feet belonged to hermits seeking anonymity, who would greatly resent being dragged into the limelight of a mercilessly inquisitive age.

Our aim is to provide the traveller abroad, should he wish to deepen his understanding of Ireland's role in the making of Europe, with a selection of what he can expect to find. He has a wide choice as to where to go. Patience and perseverance are needed, for the imprints of those tireless 'wanderers in Christ' will lead him off the beaten track. Time allowing, he can peer into a library or a monastic scriptorium of fame, where manuscripts are kept that bear testimony. He can experience the living memory of an Irish patron saint in a folk procession, or on a pilgrimage. He can stand before a sarcophagus and ponder on the lighted candles that vouch for this abiding devotion. He can marvel at the splendour of many a priceless shrine. He can also visit wells famed for their healing qualities, and explore forest caves that echoed the prayers of a lonely recluse. Climbing a height, he may then look down on a wide country that same Irish hermit christianized.

This is an Irish heritage and ours for the taking. Covering a wide field, much research needs to be done. What quality had the Irish Mission that made it so prestigious? The answer is simple: it was a mobile apostolate, and one of compassion. Arriving on the Continent in a period of change, confusion and human misery, the Irish put charity first. Beside their cells they built oratories and, annexed to these, shelters. Hermitages with hospices developed, the first of their kind to afford asylum. The common man found sympathy and was taken into the Christian fold. In return, these aliens were given a sanctuary in the very heart of the people; one so enduring that in later times priests

9

were tempted to heighten the esteem of a local saint in the eyes of the community by fitting him or her out with a pedigree of far-off 'Scotia'.

Another important factor was Irish asceticism. Spiritual contemplation being part of his discipline, the hermit shunned no danger, often accepting martyrdom as the price to be paid for a retreat in the wilds. This immolation brought people face to face with human sacrifice at its purest. Reports of miracles that ensued are nothing less than thirst for divine consolation.

In a land of ecclesiastical ruins such as Ireland, it is not hard to envisage those early days when 'churches were dark and hearts were bright', as a German historian put it. 'But now,' he added ruefully, 'churches are bright and hearts are dark.' Aventinus was writing in the 16th century, when lofty edifices had long since replaced the narrow, dark, clammy sanctuaries our *peregrini* filled with light. New saints, fashionable in Rome, were thrust on the people.

Then, as if to ban mysticism completely, the baroque period took over, bringing a haughty accent into the churches, proclaiming lustfully and gaudily their doctrinal triumph. Further and further away we drift from that humble core, from the essential creed. Even when remembered and remodelled in the hands of an artist of note, your Irish saint, smothered in gold and silver drapings, seems sadly out of place.

Nevertheless, the baroque artist was a faithful recorder and iconographically sound. An Irish saint, banished from the altar of the church he probably founded, can usually be identified in whatever corner, crypt or country chapel he may have landed. An open book in his hand identifies the evangelist or man of learning. A pack animal in his company recalls the hard manual labour involved in creating a monastic settlement. A wild beast at the saint's knee indicates the dangers of lonely regions. A dragon, or devil in chains, at his foot is a sign reserved mainly for early pioneers combating the Antichrist. The staff, or Irish *cambutta*, grasped in the right hand, denotes his travels and the itinerant nature of his ministry; if this is a crozier, it reveals his standing as a bishop, abbot, or that vague generalization, *episcopus vagans*. And should the saint have lost his life serving the Cause, he will be given a sword, axe, rope, or whatever deadly instrument was involved. Women are often given the palm of martyrdom to hold, transformed into the palm of victory.

But all that iconography can offer is tokens of respect. The *peregrinus* remains an enigma, his inner motivation a source of wonder to all ages. He will, no doubt, continue to evade us. But we can visit his haunts, where, when listening to his story, we should condescend to keep an open mind. Too readily today legends are brushed aside, and with them their historical substance. Yet how often has our oldest recorder, lore, silenced its critics!

In the ancient city of Regensburg on the river Danube, the friendship of the prelates Alabert and Erhard came to be regarded as pure fantasy, their Irish background refuted because of their germanized names; until the day when under the church of Niedermünster their Merovingian tombs were discovered side by side . . .

So much of man's heritage has gone down in the havoc he created, the havoc he calls history. Yet tradition persists, a vault of broken tombs to which he stubbornly clings. In an age of rationalism it is a legacy we cannot afford to lose.

In the spiritual life of this planet the Irish *peregrinatio* was by no means the transient affair many would have us believe. A phenomenon, pristine as a shooting star, it embodied such propulsive energy and irradiated in such a manner that only the supernatural could explain it. A later generation found this to be unacceptable. Nothing irritates the modern observer more than something that resists analysis, that will not fit into some tidy compartment of his mind. Ignoring the prestige the *peregrinus* won by the 7th century in his own land, and the high status granted him in Irish law tracts, scholars nowadays tend to decry the whole scenario as irrational, and indeed negligible, putting a question mark against the missionary commitment and even the authenticity of these Irish saints.

The traveller should not worry. As a feature of Christian society emerging in post-Roman Europe the position of the Irish Mission is secure. The key part it played is evident everywhere, just as it was recorded of old; it is far too deeply ingrained to become more than superficially submerged. A little sounding will bring it to the surface and teach us to honour the memory of man.

Decline came naturally to the movement when, at the turn of the 8th century, Charlemagne was accorded the Imperial crown in Rome. With

11

this the Western world found its bearing; a period of stabilization set in. The mobile evangelist, having served his purpose, became a thing of the past, the Irish sage now taking his place seated in palace schools and at the court of German rulers.

Alas, our knowledge of the *peregrinus* has been further blurred by neglect. The Italian order of Benedict of Nursia, having gained predominance in the West, chose to forget his merits, obliterating on occasion his very traits. Given the enormous influence of monastic institutes on the cultural life of the Middle Ages, this blank disavowal has left us with a void. The growing popularity of the Benedictine rule – being less austere than that of Columban – coalesced with the power politics of the Holy See, for Rome was intent on bringing the Carolingian Empire to heel and holding it under its control. One measure taken was the 8th-century imposition of the Roman rite rendering Gallic and Irish liturgical books obsolete. The Celtic church and its protagonists, the missionaries prized by the foregoing Merovingians, were moreover the butt of a campaign pursued acrimoniously by the Pope's legate, Wynfrith-Boniface, himself a product of Irish monastic training in Anglo-Saxon England.

Meanwhile the *peregrinus* awaits the homage that is his due. We hope in these pages to make a small contribution in that direction – and to follow, in a later volume, the traces of the early Irish Mission in Switzerland, Italy and further afield.

MEROVINGIAN GAUL

From remote antiquity Ireland was involved in the maritime exploits of the West. The Irish of the Early Christian period, hailing from a land of dense forests and wide rivers, gave preference to transport over inland waterways. Arriving at continental ports in the wake of traders following Atlantic trade routes of pre-historic times, it was natural for them to continue this practice. For those risking sea crossings in smaller boats — and we hear a lot about them — landing-places were available in sheltered bays along the rugged coastal shelf. Pilgrims then followed the eastward course of rivers from their estuaries, while anchorites settled on their wooded banks, when given the choice.

There the Irish encountered a scale of disorder unlike anything their island sanctuary offered. The breakdown of Roman rule had left a vacuum in the province of Gaul, once so exemplary, that cried out for spiritual guidance and regeneration. Into this void the so-called Celtic Church stepped — accidentally, one might add, for it is clear that supporters of that church were often merely pilgrims en route to the Holy Land or visitors to the tomb of Saint Martin in Tours. Some were priests, others monks under a penitential obligation seeking retirement from the world, intent only on the salvation of their own souls.

It so happened that a number of these 'wanderers in Christ', as they have been rightly called, became arrested by the conditions they encountered. Again and again we are told of pilgrims changing plans in face of the plight of those who begged them to stay; a fact that illustrates the failure of the rump of Roman or Celto-Roman church dignitaries to cope with the situation in Gaul. The only officials left in the country, these bishops had to take over duties beyond their calling — a task they were not up to, living as they did in splendid isolation behind their city walls. It is not surprising that there was a general relapse into paganism, a retrogression hastened by pressure from Germanic tribes in the North and East — themselves heathens or, at best, Arian heretics condemned by Rome. Arianism, flooding Europe in the 4th century, came in the wake of those Goths and Vandals who engulfed southern Gaul.

Change was brought about by Chlodwig (Clovis), king of the Salic

The baptism of Clovis I in Rheims, in a 14th-century French miniature.

Franks, who invaded northern Gaul in the late 5th century. Proclaiming that he would adopt the Faith if he won the battle of Tolbiac against the heretic Alemanni, Clovis was baptized, together with his court and his victor army, by bishop Remigius on Christmas Day, 497. His triumph in repulsing the Alemanni was attributed to the intercession of Saint Martin of Tours.

Clovis' conversion marks the rise of a new Europe, bringing the Franks to a position of predominance in the West. For a period of 250 years his Merovingian dynasty was to hold sway — crudely enough, admittedly, but with a real determination to establish the principles of Christian teaching in its expanding realms.

One result of this triumph of the Catholic Faith over Arianism was appreciation for the values of untainted Irish monasticism, its discipline, assiduity and social commitment. Clovis and his sons spared no efforts in engaging the service of its agents, inducing them to settle with generous offers of land. For a time it seemed as if the Irish element was the only stabilizing factor in this wild Merovingian world-in-the-making. Especially in exposed places they are to be found, along the Empire's fringe and sometimes beyond, tilling the soil, clearing the forests, draining the swamps and combining hospitality with teaching within the precincts of their hermitages. These being soon overcrowded, new monastic buildings arose, well donated and under royal protection.

Incarceration was, of course, not to an Irishman's liking. We find them constantly breaching monastery walls, pouring out in all directions. If such missionary zeal seemed erratic to its contemporaries, as it no doubt did, in retrospect it is equally hard to keep pace with. Were it not for its extraordinary success, few would have endeavoured to unravel a matter of such complexity.

But then again, the Merovingian period is itself one of extreme confusion, encompassing the painful changeover from Antiquity to Christendom. These Islanders, with no such transitional problems to tackle at home, came as harbingers of a new era. The marvel was that they were present when needed, grappling with odds and rising to the occasion like a good midwife. They arrived seemingly unprompted, as if answering a call from afar. Practising more than preaching, their approach was fresh and unassuming, and they moved among the people much as they considered Christ must have done. Their message was one of mercy and of hope. It was exactly what the situation needed.

14

Clovis' first royal seat in northern Gaul was Rheims, and Remigius – the apostolic Saint Remi of French history – was his bishop. With the moral backing of Rome, he could now wage wars in the name of Christendom. But Clovis was an astute ruler, and he set out to put his own house in order first. With monastic practices in the hands of Irish evangelists, the administration of the dioceses was a domestic affair calling for attention. The bishops, with their strong secular ties, were few and far between, and needed reinforcements in the North.

Ligugé. The 16th-century abbey today.

Clovis subjected Aquitaine, then a large territory south of the Loire, in 507–8. This gave him access to a still intact, if vestigial framework of society, that of the literati and the episcopate, representatives of a superior civilization, left behind at the end of Roman occupation in 476. These Gallo-Romans, hanging on to old seignorial rights, Clovis proceeded to exploit. Far from wishing to disturb their Roman order or diminish their magistrative powers the king involved them in his reforms by transferring a number of bishops from Aquitaine to the centre of his administration north of the Loire. And among those answering the call there were some of Irish extraction, or at least with Irish connexions – *ex Scottorum genere*, as we are told.

To understand the early influx of Irish into Gaul, two things should be borne in mind. First, the tremendous appeal Saint Martin had for the Celtic world. This bishop of Tours, dying in 397 or 400, was responsible for a steady flow of pilgrims into Aquitainian ports such as those of the Loire and Gironde estuaries. Pilgrimages to Tours were no less popular than those to Rome and the Holy Land. Irish monks visited the haunts of Saint Martin, seeking inspiration in the eremitic cells carved out of the cliffs at Marmoutier, and were awed by the saint's original monastery, Ligugé, the first of its kind in Gaul, founded near Poitiers in 360. The shrine of that great Christian leader in Tours, a national monument of Gallo-Romans and newly converted Franks alike, was also a source of fascination for people of the Celtic Fringe, and Irish hagiography attached to the resort such famous names as Pádraig, Colmcille, Ciarán Saighir and Ninian.

Putting these pious intentions aside, there was another motivation for Irish voyagers. Southern Gaul was a haven for the scholar. Sharing the Celtic love of classical literature and learning, Irish students were drawn to the land where this was still cultivated, seeking contact with schools of Grammar and Rhetoric, whether secular or not. In Toulouse

15

Merovingian tombs, Civaux. Remainder of an immense necropolis, reputedly for the fallen of Clovis' army in the battle of 507 near Poitiers.

and Poitiers such schools were still flourishing in the early 6th century when Clovis arrived to put the country south of the Loire under some sort of Germanic order other than that of the heretic Visigoths. And if Poitiers signified Hilarius for Irish scholars, the teachings of that great master (who led a campaign against Arianism) were hardly less popular in Ireland than those of Honoratus and Cassianus, from Lérins and Marseille respectively.

Clovis the Great conquered the Visigoths in a battle near Poitiers in the year 507. That Irish visitors very soon became involved in Clovis' programme for the conversion of the Visigoths is demonstrated in the case of Fridolin.

This intrepid *peregrinus* began his continental career in Poitiers, and we recall him when viewing the noblest sanctuary of that historic city, the basilica of Saint-Hilaire-le-Grand, built on the site of the abbey of Saint Hilarius, over which Fridolin presided. This abbey in its turn superseded the sepulchral church of its patron, Poitiers' great theologian, who became the town's first bishop in 350. Hilarius was Fridolin's ideal.

Two centuries later it was Fridolin who carried, in Saint Hilary's name, the campaign against Arianism into the farthest corners of the Franconian Empire.

Ireland lost sight of Fridolin, until in the 17th century the Franciscans caught up with him in German-speaking districts of ancient

16

Alemannia. Inclusion of his name in missals, liturgies and church calendars of his adopted countries testify that people had long ago taken this apostle to their hearts. Father Seán Mac Colgan then gave Fridolin ample space in his Louvain hagiography.

Not until the 10th century did Fridolin find a biographer. This was Baltherus, a monk of Helera (Eller, an abbey on the river Mosel) who recorded from memory such knowledge as had been passed down about the founder abbot. What had been stored in the minds of men was the tradition of a saint arriving as a pilgrim 'from the extremities of Lower Scotia, called Hybernia, that borders the ocean', who assisted Clovis, the Franconian king, in reforming the Visigoths of Aquitaine, who were addicted to heretical beliefs.

We are furthermore provided with the following story to explain the sudden promotion of a foreigner to the abbatial seat of Saint-Hilaire in Poitiers:

Arriving from Ireland, Fridolin is shocked to find the sepulchral church of Saint Hilarius vandalized by the Goths and abandoned. He spends nights in prayer amid the ruins. In a vision it is revealed to him where the holy patron lies buried beneath the rubble, and with Fridolin's instructions the lost tomb is brought to light with much rejoicing. Upon which the bishop of Poitiers offers the abbacy of the adjoining priory to Fridolin, who proceeds to restore the church and re-install in it the relics of Saint Hilarius (burned later by Calvinists).

Basilica of Saint-Hilaire-le-Grand, Poitiers.

La chapelle des Vierges, Ste-Maure-de-Touraine.

Reliquary of 'Maure et Britta' in the same church.

Fridolin's life-long obsession with Saint Hilary enables us to trace his footsteps abroad. Everywhere on his wide travels the churches he founded are, in most cases, still dedicated to the saint of Poitiers. In them Fridolin deposited relics of Hilarius, throughout the valleys of Mosel and Rhein, in Burgundy, Alsace, Switzerland and southern Germany. There we will meet him again.

On an old pilgrim route connecting Poitiers with Tours, on a height above the river Manse stands the church of Sainte-Maure-de-Touraine. This should not be passed by pilgrims of today without saluting its patrons 'Maure et Britta', over whose tombs the church was built.

These virgin martyrs from Ireland find mention in Gregory of Tours' late 6th-century History of France. They met their fate here in the forest, after praying at the tomb of Saint Martin in Tours. This happened around the year 570, when the sisters were on a return journey from Rome, accompanied by their brother Espain, who shared their martyrdom and is buried in Saint-Épain, a small town nearby. According to one tradition, they were the children of 'Ailill, king of Scotia' (that is, Ireland), and were victims of an attack by 'barbarians from the North'.

The little town of Nogent-les-Vierges derives its title from the claim that the mutilated bodies of these Irish pilgrims were first laid out there. But some church historians have confused their story with those of name-sakes such as the 9th-century Sainte Maure of Troyes, and the Irish twins belonging to the party of Saint Ursula massacred in Cologne in the 4th or 5th century. These twins were revered in various dioceses of the Rhineland in the Middle Ages, when distributions of relics for new parish churches were requested, and legends in support of candidates entered the sphere of fantasy.

Gregory of Tours was, however, a serious historian, even if the popularity of the Irish Christian names Máire and Brígit is misleading, and for a certainty a great cult developed along the Manse valley after posthumous miracles were reported at the graves of the Irish girl-martyrs he mentions, whose feastday is celebrated in January. The character of the old church on the hill was spoiled by restoration carried out in 1866, but the crypt and a chapel survived. The town itself is of Roman origin, fortified and with a castle (plate 9).

Eight kilometres north-west of Sainte-Maure lies Saint-Épain, its patron portrayed in a stained-glass window of the church, and to the north-west again we reach the hamlet of Saint-Patrice on the right bank of the Loire – it, too, with a store of legends surrounding it. One wonders what else of Irish interest remains to be discovered in the locality.

By the time Columban's influence made itself felt in the 7th century in the Poitou and in the Loire valley, Irish monks had already infiltrated many monasteries of the district. Soon they were to have houses of their own, Ansoald, bishop of Poitiers, being their great promoter. He restored the abbey of Mazerolles to cater for the Irish pilgrims in Aquitaine, placing it under the guidance of the Irish bishop Ronan (Roman). He endowed Columban's follower Philibert with an island for a monastic settlement at the mouth of the Loire. This once important religious centre, Noirmoutier, is a picturesque site, now connected to the mainland with a bridge. We hear accounts of an Irish ship bringing goods, including shoes, to the monastery in early times; no doubt they also discharged human cargo.

Other Columban monasteries of influence that arose in 7th-century Aquitaine are centred around Poitiers, the old frontier town— Civaux, Quinçay, Nouaillé, St-Cyran and, further up the Loire, Fleury. Like Quinçay, Fleury was re-named Saint-Benoît, after the remains of Saint Benedict were brought there at the end of the 7th century. Fleury has important Carolingian remains; other Columban foundations have Merovingian crypts to explore, and old monastic walls can still be traced in many places.

Modern scholars may ridicule the idea of Mansuetus, the 4th-

St-Benoît-de-Quinçay. The cloisters today.

Nouaillé abbey, with ancient fortifications, Romanesque church and crypt.

Detail of church window, St-Épain, showing the patron saint.

19

Noirmoutier. Crypt of the Merovingian foundation and tomb of St Philibert.

century missionary of the Rhône valley who became the first bishop of Toul, being identical with the Irish Mansuy (called 'Fethgno' in the Martyrology of Donegal), although this is attested in copies of early sources, such as that provided by the 10th-century bishop Adso. But we have no cause to doubt the origin of Irish dignitaries such as Toimene and Ronan, endowed with bishoprics in Angoulême and Mazerolles in the 7th century. Nor can Falvius (Failbhe?) be ignored, the bishop whose conversion of Sigiramni, honoured in Bourges as 'Saint Cyran', led to the foundation of royal abbeys of distinction. Nor, for that matter, is there reason to question the presence on the banks of the river Lot of the Irish *peregrinus* Arnán and his friendship with Desiderius of Cahors. Our query should rather be, how many more of them were there, that are lost to memory? For those interested in Mansuy, his relics are kept in the cathedral of Toul, near Nancy. In Nancy's Musée Historique he is portrayed as a worker of miracles by the famous 17th-century artist Jacques Callot.

To return to Clovis' conversion in 497, we have already news of Irish *peregrini* working with Remigius in northern France at the turn of that century, some drawn there by that bishop's fame, others arriving perhaps under pressure from Brittany. Trickling in in small groups they are allotted missionary stations in the Rheims diocese, as well as in those of adjoining Laon and Soissons. Along the Marne and Aisne valleys there were forests enough for secluded locations, but these were also haunts of *pagani* of various tribes, resenting interference. Martyrdom soon became a grim reality for those straying too far afield.

Several lives that were recorded have come down to us, as well as a names-list of a prolific Irish group, including Gibrian, who left his name on Saint-Gibrien on the Marne, and Tressan, anointed by Saint Remi, who founded the abbey of Avenay nearby, where he apparently reared swine. A certain German, godson of Saint Germanus of Auxerre(?), laboured in the valley of the Bresle near Amiens. A so-called 'regional bishop', he was martyred there and laid to rest in the present Saint-Germain-sur-Bresle, where tradition honours him as slayer of a seven-headed dragon! Tressan's relics were long honoured in Pont-aux-Dames in Brie. Those of Gibrian, brought to Rheims cathedral, were

20

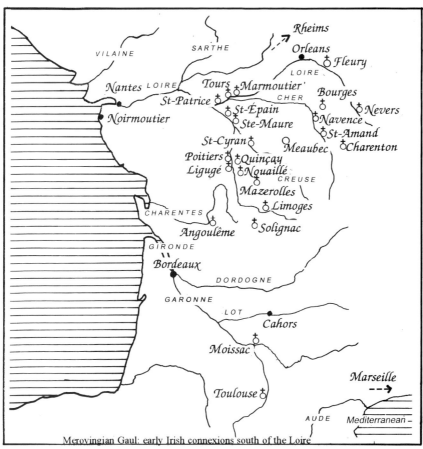

Merovingian Gaul: early Irish connexions south of the Loire

scattered and lost in the French Revolution. But place-names are faithful recorders of early cults and not easy to erase.

When phenomena of a supernatural kind came to be reported from the graves of these strange hermits, oratories and churches were erected around them to accommodate supplicants and pilgrims, and eventually Augustinian canons were settled there. Vailly, Avenay, Beaumont and Saint-Gibrien are just a few such places, standing to remind us of the activities of these avant-garde associates of Saint Remi. Later on, the Church of Rome was glad to have their cults to fall·back on, when general devotion waned. In the case of two Irish saints who were buried in the monastery of Chaumont-sur-Marne, indulgences were granted later in the Middle Ages by

21

Laon. 17th-century engraving by Matthäus Merian. The single spire in the centre is that of St-Pierre-le-Viel. Below it, walled in, the abbey of St-Vincent.

popes and cardinals to those visiting the shrines of 'Bertold and Amandus'.

In Laon these pioneers were held in great esteem, propagated by the 9th-century colony of Irish scholars headed by Eriugena, who had their quarters in the precincts of that ancient citadel, as well as their church, Saint-Pierre-le-Viel – destroyed in the French Revolution and all its contents lost. Visitors to Laon will sadly find no further reminder of this location than an alley bearing the name *rue des Scots*. But they will be comforted to find many Irish documents treasured in the municipal library.

And Laon remembers. On 1 February the 'Feast of All Hermit-Saints of Ireland' is celebrated. On the call-list are two virgin martyrs who probably belonged to the Gibrian group mentioned above – Sainte Preuve (Proba, Prompta), and Sainte Germaine (Grimona, Germana) who was murdered in the forest of Thiérache that skirts the

22

Ardennes, on the present Belgian border. Miracles occurring at Germaine's grave led to a chapel being built over it, hence the place-name 'La Capelle', for long a popular pilgrim resort. In 1540 Germaine's remains were removed to the Augustinian abbey church of Henin-Liotard (now Henin-Beaumont), together with relics of her friend and compatriot Preuve. The head of Saint Preuve was venerated by the Irish of Laon in Saint-Pierre-le-Viel.

Preuve is the earliest Irishwoman to have left a deep and lasting impression on France. Her stone effigy with two Irish monks kneeling before her has graced the west façade of Laon's great cathedral since 1200. Manuscripts in the municipal library include an antiphonary of 1210–20 recording her feastday and confirming offices held in her honour in the diocese. Also a text of the early 12th century there relates Preuve's story. Slain in the valley beneath the citadel – in the shadow of Saint Vincent's abbey that was to nurture many Irish missionaries – Preuve, decapitated, carried her head in her hands up the hill and into the church of Saint-Pierre-le-Viel, where she placed it on a stone behind the altar. The stone was still shown in the 12th century, when the account was given. A strange tale, yet highly reminiscent of Irish literary traditions!

To the north-east of Laon, where we find a lonely hamlet dedicated to Sainte Preuve, a crossroads directs us across the wet-lands of 'Le Marais Saint-Boetien' to the village of Pierre-pont, with a fine church dedicated to an Irish recluse of Saint Vincent's abbey in Laon, and one of its 'hermit-saints'. Saint Boetien (Boetius – Boathán?) was slain when missioning here in 668. His hermitage, which became the abbey of Pierrepont, of which no vestige remains, stood near a bridge the Romans built across the marches of the river Souce – hence the name 'Pierre pont', the stone bridge. Boetien was called by the people 'Saint Haillard' – the 'Saint of the Marshes' that he tried to drain, *haie* being the Gallic name for a swamp. The fame he once enjoyed is reflected in the *Chansons de Geste*, where he finds mention as 'Saint Haillard'.

Pierrepont abbey is gone, but the saint's church of the Romanesque period is worth a visit. The importance of this ancient site and its monastery is evident in vestiges of a fortified mansion, dating from the 8th-9th century, which belonged to the bishops of Laon.

Shrine of St Preuve in the church of St-Martin, Henin-Beaumont.

23

Flodoard, canon in Rheims in the early 10th century, left us valuable records of his own prestigious bishopric. He witnessed the *translatio* of the relics of Saint Gibrian from the village chapel to the abbey of Saint-Remy, and provides us with further revealing details concerning those *peregrini* that Remigius so favoured, and the hazardous conditions under which they toiled. Précord (Praecordus), slain on the banks of the Aisne, from where his corpse was carried back to Rheims by his friends, to be buried in the church of Saint-Hilaire, is first on the list of Irish hermit-saints commemorated so faithfully in Laon each February. (See map on page 45.)

BRITTANY

The Irish peregrini, *as Brittany saw them.*

Nowhere in continental Europe can we look for a more authentic picture of the Irish *peregrini* than in Brittany, for it was here that they first set foot. Stored in the minds of a conservative indigenous people was an image, still potent when the oldest wooden effigies that have survived were made. With their big pilgrim hats, bland features, and heavy cloaks and staffs, we get an impression that may well apply to Gibrian's group and others who left their mark first on Brittany, before turning their attention to the diocese of Rheims. They have certainly left their names – albeit corrupt – on the parishes of Saint-Helan, Saint-Abram, Saint-Veran and more, while their route leads back into Cornwall, the traditional place of transit for Irish voyagers in light seacraft, preferring, as they did, to cross over the head of the peninsular rather than brave the currents around Land's End.

Arriving often in Armorica, as Brittany was then called, in the company of refugees fleeing Anglo-Saxon expansion in Britain, came Irish monks who had previously sojourned in the great Welsh abbeys of Miniu, Llanildut, and Llancarfan. If commuting was habitual between flourishing Celtic monasteries of the 6th century, this obviously provided the stimulus for combined missionary ventures, such as that of the Welshman Pol (Paulus Aurelius) crossing over to Armorica together with the Irish bishop Connoc. That such groups found much of the northern coast of this former Celto-Roman maritime province

The Church of St-Thégonnec.

abandoned was due to Saxon raids, its inhabitants having fled inland. Left to the mercy of both land- and sea-robbers, many *peregrini* moved on into northern Gaul.

Those missionaries that braved it often found off-shore islands suitable as a base. Pol, arriving with Connoc around the year 530, first founded a monastery on Batz. That he did so by banishing a dragon is indicative of the pagan relapse he was confronted with.

Moving on to the mainland of Finistère, Pol takes refuge in a forsaken Roman coastal fort, the confines of which form the core of the present town of Saint-Pol-de-Léon, with the episcopal seat he founded. Pol's friend Connoc, in the meantime, ventures inland to create what is now one of Brittany's main pilgrim and tourist attractions – the monastery of Saint-Thégonnec, consisting today only of its church and surrounding *enclos paroissial*. Saint-Thégonnec became one of the richest parishes in the region, possessing a majestic Renaissance court with a calvary beside the church dating from 1610. The foundation legend is carved into the granite base of the edifice – a wolf harnessed to a truck loaded with stones. This was the act of penance imposed on the wolf by Connoc for having dared to devour the saint's horse: the wolf was condemned to bring building material to the monastery site. Saint-Thégonnec has also conserved a remarkable 'chapelle Sainte-Brigitte', honouring Ireland's patron saint.

Calvary (1610) in the grounds of St-Thégonnec.

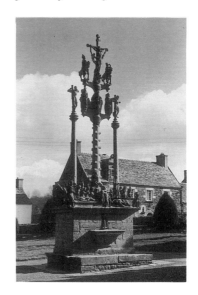

25

St Efflam and the dragon in the church of Plestin-les-Grèves.

A 16th-century effigy of St Enora, Plestin-les-Grèves.

Between Saint-Pol-de-Léon and Saint-Thégonnec lies Saint-Vougay with its 16th-century parish church that boasts an 11th-century breviary and an Irish founder called Vouga (Vio) of such extraordinary spiritual resources that when necessary he appeased the raging seas beating the coast of Finistère.

In Plestin-les-Grèves, to the east of Saint-Thégonnec, we encounter one of the most legendary and archaic Irish patrons, portrayed in the church thrusting his crozier down the throat of a dragon. This is Efflam, an Irish prince who is believed to have died in Brittany in the year 512 in the monastery he founded. His elaborate 16th-century tomb is admired here, and the well is pointed out that was conjured up by Efflam to quench King Arthur's thirst after that hero's vain attempt to master the dragon. These and more strange symbolical tales emerge out of folk memory, depicting a man who renounced title and riches and a beautiful wife in Ireland, to sail away on a *peregrinatio* of no return.

Enora, Efflam's virginal bride, also finds portrayal in the church of Plestin. She followed him to Brittany, crossing over in a leather coracle, and died in a cell that Efflam built for her beside his hermitage. The sanctity of this eremitic community is conveyed in the report of a host of angels arriving in the bay of Lannion four times a week to supply the Irish anchorites with victuals.

Efflam's great popularity and the intensity of his cult is also borne out by the incantations the saint is alleged to have uttered when rescuing Arthur from the dragon's clutches. This became a prayer to be chanted in times of peril and distress, notably in encounters with devilish spirits intent on ruining the country. And no wonder! The convergence of dragon, hero and saint on the shore called the *Lieue de Grève* is surely the most spectacular, and symbolically the most intriguing, of Brittany's inexhaustible store of dragon myths.

Having accosted the beast near its coastal den, Arthur fights for three days in an effort to slay it. Parched with thirst, he is near death when Efflam appears in the bay of Lannion, sailing over from Ireland. The dragon, maimed and stupefied at the mere sight of such a holy man, attempts to retreat backwards into his den – still to be seen! – while Efflam refreshes Arthur with a spring of sweet water. He then drags the beast out into the deep, drowning it off the 'Red Rock' that stands in the bay.

From Efflam's hermitage near the spring the work of evangelization

26

Old snapshot of a supplicant at St Efflam's well.

Modern fresco in the chapel of St Efflam showing the saint and his seven Irish companions – all named.

proceeds. Here the saint dies and is buried in his church, henceforth a great centre of pilgrimage, even after a 10th-century duke of Brittany builds a new and nobler abode for the patron's remains – the church of Plestin-les-Grèves – further inland. There Efflam has since lain.

Of his hermitage nothing remains but the name of a busy seaside resort, Saint-Efflam, to the left of which along the shore we come to the chapel of the saint, later erected in the gorge of Toul Efflam near his holy well. Both edifices have plaques to commemorate their history, inserted by the Centre Culturel de Plestin-les-Grèves. Beneath its 17th-century dome, conserved as a historical monument, the 'Fontaine de Saint-Efflam' still flows, an oracle consulted by generations, guarding the wide bay of Lannion. Even more arresting is a site on the sandy expanse of the Lieue de Grève that fills in at high tide. This is a high granite cross of indeterminable age, traditionally marking the spot where Efflam landed – and planted there by him. It was knocked over in 1944 by Allied forces landing in the bay, leaving only a stump. But in 1993, with much pomp and ceremony, a television crew and three thousand onlookers, the *Croaz an Hanter Lew*, 'The Mid-way Cross', was re-installed (plate 13). May it again fulfil its divine duties, in saving

Cloister ruins at St-Malo's medieval cathedral.

the lives of those attempting to cross the sands of the League's breadth on a path of antiquity, taken by Romans and Celts before them — a path used down to our times, when a coastal road, that now skirts the bay, was built to suit modern traffic.

Until then it was on Efflam's 'Half-way Cross' the traveller had to fix his attention. If its base was found to be damp and dark he had no choice but to turn back, or continue on and drown in the incoming tide before reaching the opposite coast. Likewise, when sea fog set in, anyone crossing the League's invisible path was guided by chimes of the 'Bell of Sainte Enora' from the shore. Still to be seen is the ancient granite belfry jutting out at Kerallic near the holy well and called 'la noguette de sainte Enora' — Efflam and Enora! magical names that rang through the ages, Irish voices of hope for souls in distress!

The new road brought tourism to Trégor; Plestin and Saint-Efflam prospered. But as everything in this world has its price, this put an end to the colourful feastday processions that nourish the Breton's heart. However, hundreds still follow the steps of their forebears and brave the traffic in order to reach these coastal sanctuaries and pray at the well and at the chapel of their Irish patron, especially on Pattern Day, the 'Great Pardun of Saint Efflam', 5 June.

Much as the subject is tempting, we cannot afford to dwell longer on these apostles of northern Finistère and the land of Trégor, but will proceed eastward along the coast of what is now the Département of Côtes-du-Nord, where Irish infiltration is noticeable mostly in place-names. This sector includes the Emerald Coast, that reaches out beyond the gulf of Saint-Malo, where Aleth (now Saint-Servan) saw generations of Irish pilgrims come and go — or come to stay.

It was near Plouba that Brioc and Budoc landed. The latter, son of a Breton fugitive in Ireland, built his first monastery on the Islet of Lavret beside the Island of Bréhat, some traces of which are visible. Of Saint Brioc, as of Saint Tugdual, so many contradictory traditions regarding his background exist that a definite conclusion seems out of reach. Such vagaries confirm generally the remoteness of the period under review, and we have to accept them, as in the case of Brioc (Breac) and Tugdual (Tuathal), patron saints of Saint-Brieuc and Tréguier, who are in some way connected. An early Life of Brioc presents him as son of

28

an Ulster ruler, settling in Brittàny after completing a Rome pilgrimage. To assume that he is identical with the famous Brychan, who left his name on Breconshire, is hypothetical but not impossible.

Tugdual, also called Pabo, enjoys the patronage of one of Brittany's impressive cathedrals, Saint-Tugdual in Tréguier, where we can admire him, bearing a bishop's tiara, a chained dragon at his side.

Bridge spanning the Rance near Dinan, where Vouga jumped.

Predominant in folk memory along the Emerald Coast is the arrival of another party of seven, the loosely defined 'Seven Holy Brothers from Ireland', to whom Saint-Cast, Saint-Briac, Saint-Lunaire and other places are dedicated. Said to belong to the 5th century, their tombs and effigies still grace village churches, where stone troughs on shores are pointed out as being the boats that brought them hither. Some of these holy hermits penetrated the bay of Saint-Malo (Aleth) where they explored the long-stretched fjord of the Rance river, leaving their names on Saint-Buc and Saint-Suliac. Apart from their Christian teaching, they brought with them – perhaps from the Irish abbey of Tintagel in Cornwall? – legends of Merlin and Viviane, to take root, along with those of King Arthur, in the once immense primeval forest of Brocéliande at the valley's extremity. Breton lore casts a queer pagan light on its earliest visitors of the New Faith. At the far end of the Rance fjord, a distance of twenty kilometres, lies Dinan, and the village of Lanvallay, deriving its name from an Irish monk of Landévennec abbey who – like Saint Moling with his famous leap over the Barrow – outwitted his heathen pursuers by jumping across the Rance. He landed on a rock, where the mark of his foot is shown, and taking his marvellous escape to be a sign from heaven, built there and then his hermitage – *Lann Valay*.

Saint Mac Low, later called Malo, who is sometimes counted as one of the Seven Holy Brothers, was Saint Brendan's pupil in the Welsh abbey of Llancarfan and his companion on many a sailing trip, as we know. But according to his *vita*, Mac Low was also guest of Saint Columban in Burgundy before settling down here in Brittany as bishop of Aleth. These connexions might just be possible, if we accept the given date of Mac Low's demise – 620, at the age of 110.

It is interesting to find the three great apostles belonging to the oldest stratum of Celtic Christianity on the European mainland – Brendan, Columban and Malo – brought together in legends of the Rance.

29

Monastery ruins, Landévennec.

Brendan, too, has his sanctuaries here. Alone in Trégor, churches dedicated to 'Sant Brandan' are found in Lanvellec and Trégrom – the latter claiming to possess his monolithic coffin!

Decisive for the advance of Christianity in Brittany was the establishment of two missionary centres in the Cornaouille, now Finistère. Situated near the coast, with its bays, inlets and estuaries, and orientated towards the West, they provided shelter for both pilgrims and refugees, arriving in droves from across the sea. In Landévennec, founded sometime in the 5th century, to be followed up by Daoulas around the year 500, Irish monasticism prevailed. Traffic, however, went sometimes the other way, as we learn from the Life of Landévennec's founder Guenolé, a pupil of Budoc from the Isle of Lavret. Ships took people from Armorica to safety in Ireland (where Budoc was born), evading the onslaught of post-Roman pagan tribes, and fleeing persecution. Landévennec, that arrests our attention as an imposing block of ruins, was to those Dark Ages first a refuge, then a bulwark of civilization

30

and learning, where the precepts of Columban were up-held and the Irish tonsure worn, until forbidden by Louis the Pious in 818. For centuries the office of Saint Brigid was read here, and from the monastery her cult spread.

Sacked by the Norse in 913, Landévennec was rebuilt in the 11th century, only to suffer more vicissitudes. It was last rebuilt as a monastery in the 16th century, to be finally dismantled in the French Revolution and left to decay.

In its now preserved ruins several pre-Norman parts are visible, including the base of the church apse, and stone fragments can be found ornamented with carvings of figurative Celtic design. A small museum provides information on the history of this cradle of Christian culture to which Ireland contributed so much.

The foundation-story of Daoulas is one of shame and disgrace. In the late 5th century a pagan lord of Faou, angered by the growing influence

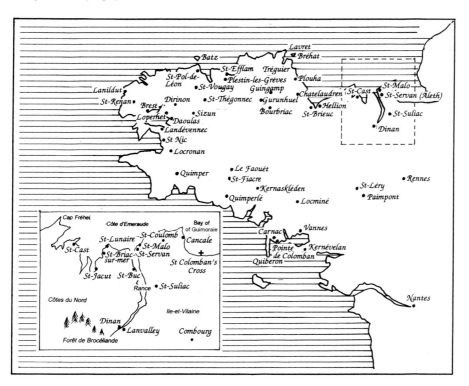

of monks settling in the Cornaouille, stormed a council held in a monastery near Landévennec, killing two abbots with his sword. This he regretted, and the act of penance imposed on him was the erection of a monastery at the scene of his crime. The legend accounts for the name of the abbey, that was to become so famous – in Breton 'Mouster Daou-las', the monastery of the two-fold murder.

As in the case of Landévennec, Irish associations with Daoulas were intense. Irish monastic observance prevailed, the tonsure was worn, and charity was practised. Well endowed, Daoulas had a hospital for victims of the plague, and a hospice for pilgrims. And like Landévennec it was forced out of existence under repeated Viking attack, until the year 1125, when the duke of Léon caused the abbey to be rebuilt for the Augustinians. Under the care of that order, Daoulas took up its old duties, and in extended and improved buildings soon regained its position as the spiritual and cultural centre of the region. It became the gathering place for pilgrims on their way to Spain; Jerusalem and the Holy Land having fallen into Arab hands, the tomb of Saint James in Santiago de Compostela was now Ireland's favourite pilgrim resort.

The last Augustinian friars were driven out of Daoulas in the French Revolution. Today the abbey's spacious ruins are under State care and open to the public. In its medieval courtyard an ancient fount, with its *têtes coupées* and geometrical designs, seems to recall

Daoulas. The original abbey wall with its stone effigies.

pagan Celtic roots. Against the pre-Norman section of the cloister's wall, two enigmatic stone figures guard an exit. The one in monkish habit might well be Columban.

In the abbey grounds is a spring, where for centuries cures were sought for eye diseases, as also for help in impending child-birth. The granite Renaissance covering is embellished with a figure of the Virgin Mary. It may be conjected that the well's original patron in Christian times was Saint Brigid, to whom such curative powers are attributed, and who has her own church nearby in Loperhet.

Dirinon. Church and sepulchral chapel of Ste Nonne.

If Brigid of Kildare never visited Brittany, the country is proud of other saintly women from Ireland who did so. Of these anchoresses none has been more treasured in memory and honoured in sanctuaries that are to be found spread throughout the land, than 'Sainte Nonne' (Non, Nonnita). Famed in Wales as the mother of Saint David, a trace of her cult is found there in the remains of the medieval Saint Nonn's church above Bride's Bay. According to legend, it was Saint Ailbhe of Emly, Nonne's nephew, who gave her protection, baptizing her child, who was born at sea, Divy (David). Tradition places Nonne therefore into the 5th or 6th century.

Nonne fled to Brittany after her violation by a Welsh lord. Here she lived and died as a recluse on the banks of the Cornaouille river Elorn. Venerated by the natives, pilgrimages to her grave in Dirinon – 'Diri-Non', the place of the nun – grew into a cult of such proportions, that in 1577, beside the church, a special chapel was built to house her remains. There, on the monolithic block of her tomb, Nonne's image is impressively carved, guarded by two angels and supported by an obedient if fiery dragon.

Legends naturally suffer a shift of accent, when saga material is passed from one Celtic land to another. In Brittany the acclaimed version is, that Nonne, Irish-born and christened Melane, gave birth to Divy on arrival here from Wales. Her abject misery is accentuated by the story of the rock that softened and curled up to form a cradle for the new-born infant, destined to become a famous saint.

On the road that leads north from Daoulas to Dirinon we pass a holy well and oratory dedicated to Sainte Nonne, and further down the road is another well, dedicated to her son Divy, the chapel of which has recently been restored. The church of Dirinon with its

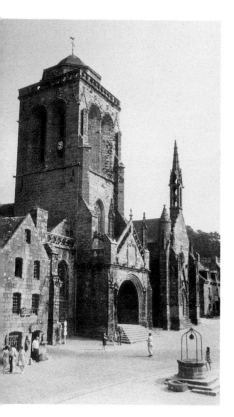

*Locronan. Church and
sepulchral chapel of
St Ronan.*

elegant Renaissance tower, beside which Sainte Nonne's chapel stands, has among many interesting features the poignant life-story of its patron portrayed in a modern window in the choir.

It has been said that there are too many saints in Brittany to be counted. They have spiritually enriched the people; what matter that Rome never recognized them? To judge by the store of legends attached to their names, it is hard to beat Saint Ronan for popularity, enjoying, as he does, unabating respect and attention. During his lifetime, however, this Irish saint had his good share of tribulations, such as envy, grudge and mistrust, known to beset the *firéin*; in fact, he barely escaped martyrdom.

The grave mistake Ronan made, was that, like Goar in the Rhineland, and Pellegrino delle Alpi in Italy, he succumbed to the urge of putting his hand-bell into charitable service. Landing on the rugged coast of Léon in his stone (!) boat, he sought out a cave on the cliff for his hermit cell. Here he practised ringing his Irish bell, in order to ward mariners off the dangerous reefs below. This act of mercy infuriated native beachcombers, a wild lot, we are told, who in their poverty depended on salvage from shipwrecks for a living. Ronan was forced to move on.

He wandered southward into the Cornouaille. There, in the depths of the druidical forest of Nevet he decided to stop. A local peasant came to his aid in setting up a modest hermitage. One day a sheep belonging to this native is snatched by a wolf, whereupon Ronan orders the culprit to return his booty. The sheep's owner, rejoicing, is now Ronan's staunch disciple, and a believer in the Word of Christ. Less delighted is his wife Keben. She spreads the news abroad that the hermit in the forest is in reality a *loup garou*, a werewolf, and should be hunted to the ground. This having no effect, Keben resorts to another plan. She hides her husband's favourite child in a chest, then pretends that it has been stolen in the night and devoured by the werewolf Ronan.

Ronan is brought before king Gradlon to answer for his deeds. Accused of sorcery and murder, he is put to the test, according to the law of the times. Two rabid wolfhounds are set on him. At the sign of the cross made by Ronan, the animals crouch meekly down at the saint's feet. The missing child is then found suffocated in the chest, and is restored to life through Ronan's prayer.

34

After his rehabilitation, Ronan performs many wonders, healing the sick and the blind, who are brought to his forest cell. For him solitude is now only attainable by the aid of an impenetrable cobweb, that visitors find from time to time spun across the cave entrance to his oratory.

The hatred of Keben has only increased, and after new intrigues the saint grows weary. He is old, and has but one wish — to return to Ireland to die. He sets out for a port near Saint-Brieuc in the North. There, on the peninsular of Hillion, Ronan expires.

Cenotaph of St Ronan in the chapelle du Pénity, Locronan.

Bishops and lords then dispute the right of interring Ronan in their respective domains. The decision is eventually left to providence. Four white oxen are to determine where the saint's remains should find a resting-place. The team makes its way over hills and dales, carrying Ronan back to the land of Cornouaille. They make a circuit of the forest of Nevet and then crash through the brush to come to a halt beside the hermit's cell.

Knowledge of this legend, depicted on the church pulpit, helps us to appreciate the extraordinary event that can be witnessed yearly in Locronan, the town that arose around Ronan's hermitage, for the path of the oxen became the route of one of Brittany's most famous and most colourful pilgrimages, a *pardun* called 'The Troménie of Locronan' — *Tro Menehi*, the tour of the hallowed ground. The yearly Troménie on the saint's feastday is a moderately small circuit, but every sixth year the 'Grande Troménie' takes place, covering a circuit of over twelve kilometres—the path taken by the white oxen. On a march, attended by people from far and wide, the procession is headed by Ronan's shrine and his holy bell, the *hirglas*, and stations are held at twelve of the twenty-four oratories along the route. The attendance of such a great concourse of pilgrims through the ages was a sacred duty, responding to the old warning: 'He who does not make the Grande Troménie in his life-time, must do so in After-life, and that at a daily pace of the length of his coffin'!

One of the stations of the Troménie is Keben's Cross. That ignoble person was doing her washing here when the oxen passed with Ronan's corpse. Throwing her beater at them in fury, she broke the horn off one of the animals. This only fell to the ground when the oxen reached the crest of a nearby hill, since called 'Plas-ar-c'horn' and crowned with a chapel. As for Keben, she was promptly swallowed up in hell's fire. A granite cross for all to see marks the spot of her descent in a blast of sulphuric smoke.

Since king Gradlon ruled Brittany around the year 475, Ronan has been dated accordingly. But an ancient breviary of the cathedral of Quimper, the capital of Cornouaille, puts him a little ahead of that time. One way or the other, it matters little, for Ronan is a living part of Brittanic lore, his name cherished in a wealth of churches and chapels around the country, and candles burn on beside his beautiful granite cenotaph in Locronan's Chapelle de Pénity.

16th-century stone effigy of St Fiachra, Lignières, Aube.

Like Saint Ronan, Fiachra is in Brittany a saint of strong local colour. Yet his cult spread through the greater part of France, where he died in the second half of the 7th century. His itinerary is obscure; dedications, such as in Les Iffs, where the well of his supposed hermitage was noted for its cures, are mainly inland, which may indicate that it was not in Brittany that he first touched continental soil, but in Normandy, to which his fiancée is supposed to have pursued him. His presence is nevertheless well attested in Brittany. Fiachra lived at a time when larger scale ventures abroad became possible. Civil upheavals, rendering royal protection and patronage ineffectual (compare Columban's zig-zag course across Gaul) were less a feature of things, when Fiachra got underway.

Devotions to Fiachra in Brittany concentrate around two places. In Morbihan, a little to the south of Le Faouët, processions are still held to the 15th-century Chapelle Saint-Fiacre. Together with that of Kernascléden, to the East, the church is a perfect example of the so-called flamboyant Gothic architecture of Brittany, boasting several belfries and very notable furnishings. How the tiny hamlet of Kernascléden came to possess its imposing church is explained by the legendary intercession of angels, attending to the construction of Saint Fiachra's church near Le Faouët. These sublime spirits, we are told, transported stonemasons together with their tools through the air on a loan to Kernascléden.

Gurunhuel, an ancient northern parish in Brittany, also has a 15th-century church dedicated to Fiachra, and if the saint did land on the peninsular it may well have been at the port of Légué (Saint-Brieuc) in the vicinity. Near Gurunhuel the old market-town of Châtelaudren lies on the axis of a Gallo-Roman trade route that would have led the Irish saint to the Paris region of northern Gaul, his ultimate destination. And in Châtelaudren there stands on a rise an early church dedicated to our Lady, in which we can admire a row of old paintings depicting the legend of Fiachra, in a side-chapel.

Near Gurunhuel again, a tall church spire is visible. This is Bour-briac, a small place still attracting pilgrims seeking relief from nervous disorders. Its patron is the Irish hermit Briac, whose bones are kept there in a sarcophagus of Merovingian design.

Whether Briac is identical with the above-mentioned Brioc, or Briac of Saint-Brieuc, is open to question – probably not. Bourbriac consid-ered that its Irish saint was the son of Tugdual, and that he founded a monastery here in which he died about the year 570.

A curiosity of Bourbriac is the cavity under the high altar of the church. Until not so long ago, persons suffering fits were locked into it for the period in which mass was celebrated above on their behalf.

Before we follow Fiachra to Paris, our attention must turn to Columban. Neither the saint in his writings, nor his biographer Jonas reveals when, where, and in what manner the apostle and his companions reached mainland Europe. Two places in Brittany contest the honour, on the north coast near Saint-Malo, and on the south coast near Vannes. We should perhaps opt for the north, where so many of Columban's forerunners steering towards the gulf of Aleth first set foot. To the east of this, in the bay of Guimoraie, stands a granite cross, recently restored (plate 17), to mark his arrival on the beach of Guesclin – a truly historic occasion of either the year 570 or 590. In a small inland village beside the bay, that claims his patronage and calls itself Saint-Coulomb, we find his image (of no ancient date).

Around the southern bay of Morbihan there is a concentration of localities bearing reference to Columban. This may have resulted from the proximity of the Loire estuary, where the story of the abortive attempt to expel the unwelcome guest, who called himself a *peregrinus,* was centred. This, of his recorded miracles the most spectacular, must have given impetus to the spread of the cult of Columban along the seaboard. Apart from that, it is quite likely that the saint visited Morbi-han, with its important seaport Vannes, where a well and a church and several topographical sites bear his name. It is under a whole mantle of distorted names that we have to search for Columban in Brittany. He is called Clomer, Coulman, Come, Colban, etc., and there, where memory failed and the cult slackened, his dedications were sometimes passed on to saints with little or no connection to the country, such as Clément and Cornély.

The 'fontaine Saint-Colomban' near Carnac, Morbihan.

Hard to determine is whether Columban was himself present in places such as Daoulas, that adhered to his principles at an early date, or if this impact was due to the prompt return of his Breton disciples from Luxeuil. Another factor to bear in mind is the constant flow of Irish pilgrims passing through. On the return from Rome via the Appenines, relics were taken from the saint's grave in Bobbio. A depository we know of for these was Locminé, to the north of the gulf of Morbihan — a great centre for the cult of Columban in Brittany, that still continues to flourish. Monks from Luxeuil had an abbey in Locminé around the year 700 that was burnt down in the 9th century. In the present-day

38

church an interesting bas-relief illustrates the expulsion of Columban by the Franconian queen Brunhilde.

Dedications, fairly distributed throughout the parishes, do seem to imply that Columban's sojourn in Armorica was, as elsewhere on his roamings, circumspect and thorough-paced; a powerful signature that did not fail to impress the Merovingian court in northern Gaul. From there – either Rheims or Orleans, depending on the period we opt for for Columban's arrival on the Continent – the king (either Sigibert or Gunthram, grandsons both of Clovis I) sent a messenger to Armorica requesting the Irishman's visit. And this, for a certainty: when setting out for the Merovingian capital, Columban had his group replenished with Breton disciples. They were to follow him on to Luxeuil.

Annegray. Chapel (museum) and part of the old wall. A cross marks the site of Columban's abbey church.

BURGUNDY

To see Annegray on its small plateau above the Breuchin valley amid the wooded slopes of the Vosges mountains is a touching sight and the Irish visitor cannot fail to be moved. Here in the vast confines of the Austrasian-Burgundian border a flame was lit that endured, enabling Europe to emerge from the void and find its own spiritual identity. Here on the Montagne de Saint-Martin was born a monastic rule destined to become the backbone of an emerging society, conceived by a stranger from beyond the Western Sea; an Irish monk armed with nothing but his vision and his pilgrim staff, but with the will and the intellect to put his convictions into action. Here in the old Roman fort known as *Anagrates*, devastated in the 5th-century Hunnish invasion and since deserted, that Rule took form. Having wandered this far, Columban and his followers found in the Vosges their footing.

What was the attraction of Annegray? Probably some means of fortification, such as the remains of a rampart or trench around the mound. Its masonry restored, the monks could hope to ward off intruders from the wild. They laboured under the direst conditions, clearing the ground for tilling and making the *castrum* habitable – often near starvation, we are told by Columban's biographer. Margaret Stokes, an Irish visitor to the site in the late 19th century, found only a ploughed field where labourers had unearthed many human bones. Excavations were begun in 1958. They brought to light both pagan and early Christian remains. Broken pillars, Roman slates, bronze statuettes, sarcophagi and part of the enclosing wall confirmed, with the bas-relief of the goddess Diana found in 1718, that Annegray was a site of worship, if not of habitation, in pre-Christian times (plate 22).

What still remains to be determined is the origin of a sanctuary dedicated to Saint Martin, that gave the locality its name. Were there christianized Romans here, before Columban arrived? More archaeological research might provide the answer.

In the centre of the compound we find now a cross, erected where stood the last church of Annegray, destroyed during the French Revolution. A small building outside the former monastery entrance, serving then as a chapel, has been converted into a museum, carefully tended to by the society of 'Les Amis de Saint Columban', based at Luxeuil (Haute-Saône).

Was Columban surprised by the success of his foundation? The space on the mound is limited. With the fame of the monastery spreading, Annegray soon burst its seams. Columban's vibrant personality, his preaching, his healing powers drew ever greater numbers to the forest resort, it seems. Another settlement was necessary to accommodate converts asking for admission. The site of Luxeuil was chosen, twelve kilometres away.

Winding its way downstream from Annegray, the river Breuchin passes the hamlet of Sainte-Marie-en-Chanois. Following a signpost directing us to 'La Grotte de St Colomban', a steep ascent (not necessarily by foot any more) ends in a forest clearing where Columban's private retreat is revered (plate 20). A true *peregrinus* needs a place to retire to, to pray and fast in quiet; Columban made this his *desertum*, at a distance of three kilometres from Annegray. Ever since, this place was the source of legends, where wolves are tamed, a bear is evicted from his den to provide the saint with an oratory, and a spring magically appears, gushing from a rock. A chapel was erected later by the people beside the famed cave. It houses the saint's stone bed, and an altar with his image. Bilberries, that grow profusely on the mountainside, are here nicknamed 'Les brinbleus de Saint Colomban', as they are reputed to have served the abbot of Annegray to appease his hunger after fasting. The spring water, serving likewise, is still bottled and prized for its healing qualities.

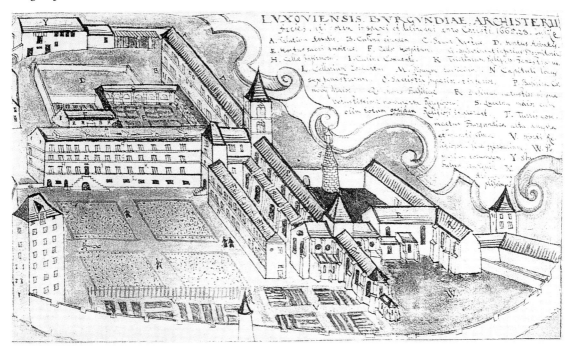

Little remains in Luxeuil to recall the Age of Columban. Too many disasters befell that monastic city. The original complex was reduced to ruins in the 8th and 9th centuries, when Saracens and Norsemen passed this way. Rebuilt, restored repeatedly after onslaughts of later centuries, the monastery was given up at last after pillage and desecration during the French Revolution, when the monks were dispersed and their splendid library, which had served so many scholars of distinction, burned to the ground.

The 20th century has seen an upsurge of common interest in Luxeuil's foundation. Conferences are held, commemorations in honour of Saint Columban are celebrated, and 1947 saw a striking statue of the saint raised to guard the entrance to the basilica of Saint Peter and Paul that stands on the site of his first abbey church.

What Columban had found there at the foot of the Vosges mountains were the ruins of Luxovium, a military station of the Romans, which because of its hot springs, was patronized by the Celts before them. Excavations of these thermal baths brought to light oaken *ex-voto* offerings of Gallic origin. This collection is displayed in the municipal

The abbey of Luxeuil, sketched in 1665.

Crest of the 'Friends of St Columban' association, showing his itinerary from Bangor, to Luxeuil, to Bobbio, with Columban's symbol, the sun.

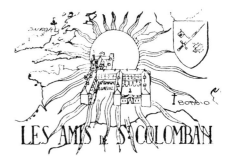

41

18th-century thermal baths at Luxeuil.

Interior of the St-Pierre, basilica, Luxeuil, built in 1330 to replace the main Columban abbey church.

museum, together with stone sculptures portraying Roman citizens. Alas, no remains of the Early Christian period have survived to bear testimony to the existence of the royal abbey of Luxeuil, the monastic capital of the 7th-century Merovingian Empire and its guiding star.

Endowed with special privileges, the monastery of Columban flourished and expanded, minting its own coinage and guarding a status of independence and immunity granted within a radius of twelve walking hours from the abbatial enclosure. Inside, among its many sanctuaries a school, a workshop and a hostel were provided, and its scriptorium took the lead in the art of illuminated manuscripts. By the middle of the 7th century Luxeuil counted 600 inmates, the number of daughter institutes and others under its guidance rising during that century to over a hundred, strewn across the face of an expanding empire. The few specimens of Luxeuil scriptoria that have come down to us are due to the utilization of Luxeuil textbooks in affiliated monasteries, thus escaping destruction when the Saracens overran Burgundy. One of these precious items, held to be the oldest existing codex of the Franconian Empire, is now in New York.

Columban was forced to leave Luxeuil in 610, but his labour bore fruit. Having set the pace, his enthusiasm proved to be contagious, and his missionary ambitions were carried out by his successors in the abbacy. The Rule, its extreme rigour often modified, soon penetrated regions north of *Gallia Belgica*, the Lowlands beyond the Somme, and across the Rhine. Over the Vosges mountains it spread through Alsace and undertook the evangelization of Bavaria. And the expelled founder himself brought the rule of Luxeuil into Switzerland and over the Alpine glaciers into Italy. The nucleus of all this is a sleepy little town of Burgundy, now in the Département Franche-Comté, once peopled with Irish monks.

In the valley of the Roge, near the main abbey, a subordinate house was set up by Columban, charged with providing the community with victuals. This is the priory of Fontaine. A walk through the woods on the road to Bourbonne will bring us to a village of that name. On the original site are the remains of a priory of later date. The parish church of Fontaine has modern dedications to the founder.

Forced to leave the country of their adoption, the Irish group and their Breton brethren were driven out of Luxeuil under military escort.

This was in answer to the fiery rebuke administered to the Austrasian royal family by Columban on moral grounds. One of the expelled, Dicuil (Desle), who had accompanied Columban from Ireland, had to be left behind on the Roman road leading from Luxeuil to Besançon, because he could go no further. Thrusting his way into the deep forest for fear of being apprehended by the militia, Dicuil meets a swineherd, who helps him find suitable cover. As he leans on his staff in exhaustion, a spring appears at the monk's feet — a sign he takes, not only for quenching his thirst, but also for building a cell there. This spring became famous. Down to the 20th century sick children were brought to 'La fontaine de Saint Desle' to profit from its reputed healing qualities.

Luckily for Dicuil, a new king takes over. This is Chlotar II, under

The expulsion of Columban from Luxeuil. Etching by Jacques Callot, 1636.

Site of Lure abbey with the 'Font de Lure'.

whose astute rule Clovis' kingdom is again united. The hermit sage in the Burgundian forest has gained such repute, that it reaches the king's ears, and when hunting there one day Chlotar witnesses the taming of a fierce boar by Dicuil. This, and the deep impression made on the king by the hermit's discourse, results in land being granted at the source of the river Reigne for the erection of a new monastery.

This is the foundation-legend of the great abbey of Lure. Famed for centuries as a seat of learning, its missionary field spread across Burgundy and into Alsace.

Part of the abbey site is today covered by a stately 18th-century building, used by the district magistrate. A large surrounding lake, containing the source of the Reigne river and called 'Le font de Lure', is a picturesque setting, such as the ancient abbey must have shared.

According to the *Vita Deicolae*, Dicuil had first missioned unsuccessfully in East Anglia, before joining Columban's party in Ulster. The Bollandist Fathers state also that he was a brother of Saint Gall, Columban's supporter on the Swiss Alemanni mission. If so, Dicuil must have been far older, for his *obit* is the year 625, after a long career. Saint Gall died around 640. The family connexion referred to may simply imply monastic brotherhood.

The small town of Lure has reason to be proud of its foundation. Since the abbey's destruction, its patron's relics have been kept in the parish church, where an old oil painting above his altar depicts the sad farewell of Columban and 'Saint Desle' on the Roman road that passed here from Luxeuil to Besançon.

NORTHERN FRANCE

Around the middle of the 7th century Fiachra puts in an appearance in northern Gaul. In the Paris region of Ile-de-France and in the adjoining Brie district, which claims him as its patron saint, we find him again, warmly welcomed by bishop Faro of Meaux on the Marne. Faro(n), of Burgundian nobility, was one of those who had received Columban's personal blessing as a child, and he greatly favoured Irish missionaries. His abbey, Sainte-Croix of Meaux, was stocked with

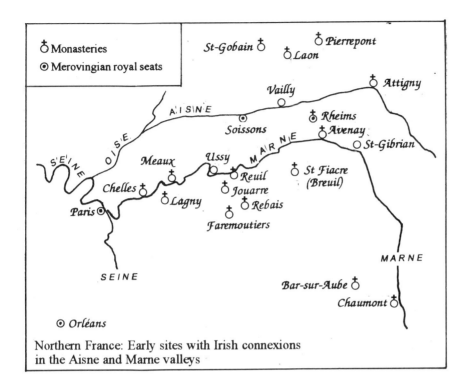

Northern France: Early sites with Irish connexions
in the Aisne and Marne valleys

Aubigny-en-Artois.
Figure of St Cilian
over the church door.

monks from Luxeuil, and Irish pilgrims found a welcome there on their
way to and from Rome, for Meaux lay on the old Gallo-Roman route
that led from the Channel coast eastward. Fiachra, arriving with his
small party from Brittany, was not alone in being attracted to Meaux; so
were others such as Cilian (Kilien, Hellien), the Irishman who was to
become patron saint of the Artois in Picardy. The two contemporaries
met in Meaux when Cilian, returning from Rome, changed his plans
and decided to stay.

Cilian's apostolate was considerable, although his *vitae*, written long
after, contain much fabulous material. We apprehend from them that
he spent long years in Rome before turning down the offer of the
papacy(!), preferring to take up the life of a wandering evangelist. The
space accorded 'Saint Kilien' in early calendars, however, leaves no
doubt as to the impact of his mission in north-eastern Gaul, a region
still predominantly heathen. Cilian's relics are in Aubigny, where he
died, honoured for his many miracles. The church is named after him
(Département Pas-de-Calais).

45

Fiachra, a hermit by nature and as such not prone to the comforts of a monastic life inside the Gallo-Roman walls of the noble city of Meaux, is allotted by Faro a place of his own to settle in, on the abbey lands of Breuil. This zone lay to the East, its vast forests considered uninhabitable, being infested with 'sorcerers' and their barbaric adherents. That it is deemed appropriate for Fiachra's vocation is no invention of his biographers in order to stress the saint's courage. Centuries later unholy practices such as the 'Witches' Sabbath' are reported in the vicinity.

There in Breuil Fiachra manages to combine the impossible – the life of an anchorite with that of a busy prior and a missionary. In the clearing he makes for himself he builds a hospice, set apart from his hermitage. This, as well as catering for pilgrims and wayfarers, acts as an asylum for the sick and needy. For their upkeep Fiachra makes the surrounding land arable, creating a huge garden where vegetables, fruit, flowers and medical herbs are grown. And he has, like Columban, his *locus deserti*, a covert beside a well in a secluded place since called 'Le bois de Fiacre'. Here in the forest of Breuil the modest abbot lives and dies, expiring around the year 670. People of all calling visit his grave in search of posthumous cures.

Briefly sketched, this is the story of Fiachra, a saint of France about whose Irish background nothing is known, except that he was of gentle birth. To get a better grasp of his personality, which must have been outstanding, we need to climb through mountains of legends.

What does iconography tell us? It gives us a humble figure in monk's attire holding a book and a spade, often a basket of fruit at his sandaled feet. Fiachra, the patron of horticulturists, has, however, an implement at his disposal that is more that a simple spade; considered so holy that it had to be buried with its master. In the oldest effigies of the saint it is not a spade at all, but an Irish *cambutta* he is holding – one with a 'Tau' head.

Whatever the case, tradition affirms that it was through the power of this instrument that Fiachra consolidated his monastic settlement. (We are reminded of angelic traditions concerning the foundation of Armagh.)

The legend of the foundation of Saint-Fiacre-en-Brie, as the abbey came to be known, is as follows:

In Breuil the concourse of pilgrims reaches such dimensions that Fiachra is obliged to make a petition to bishop Faro in Meaux for a supplementary piece of land to cater for them. Faro informs Fiachra that he can take as much land as he is able to dig around in one day. Returning to the forest, Fiachra grasps his spade and starts to mark a line for the required extension by digging a trench. The spade barely touches the ground when beneath it a deep cleft appears. Fiachra proceeds with the round, the chasm advancing with him, trees falling to the right and to the left to carve out the spade's way. Soon a wide circle is drawn, with a trench to mark the precincts of a new monastery.

This uncanny performance does not go unobserved. A busybody called in tradition 'La Becnaude' hastens away to Meaux with the news. She denounces Fiachra as a fearful sorcerer to bishop Faro. Whereupon she returns to Breuil with the bishop's order to cease all operations immediately. The Becnaude heaps insults on Fiachra, who sinks abjectly down on a forest boulder to await the arrival of Faro. And there, beside the trench the bishop finds him, but lo! the jagged surface of the rock the saint is seated on has melted, out of sympathy, into a consolatory chair! Tendered proof is a rounded, indented stone, placed beside the tomb that once held St Fiachra's remains, in the village church where his abbey once stood. Inhabitants of that village are aware of the site of the famous trench in the forest, earthworks being visible for a long time.

Overwhelmed by such signs of Fiachra's divine calling, Faro promises every assistance. It is also ordained that, since it was a woman who vilified the poor hermit, men alone should be allowed to cross the border trench. The Becnaude receives her due personally, for while Fiachra's stone turned smooth and soft as wax, her own countenance takes on the quality of a scarred, jagged rock.

A prohibition for women to set foot within the precincts of the abbey of Saint-Fiacre in Breuil existed down to its dissolution in 1760. We also note that a far stricter monastic rule was observed there, distinguishing it from the seventeen other abbeys subordinate to Sainte-Croix in Meaux which later became 'Saint-Faron'.

Up to the 9th century Fiachra's cult was limited to the locality, but by the 13th century it had become widely acclaimed and the legend glorified in many liturgical hymns. Rebuilt again and again after destruction, the abbey of the saint in Breuil with its three churches, its

17th-century silver statuette on a reliquary of St Fiachra from Chanzeaux abbey, Maine-et-Loire.

hospice, its large garden plot, was a main pilgrim resort of the people of France. Only one church has survived. It was enlarged in the 19th century to serve the parish of Saint-Fiacre, that grew up around the abbey. The parishioners are proud to welcome pilgrims and to show visitors the patron saint's image above the church door (plate 18). Within are votive tablets – only one surviving the French Revolution – which testify Fiachra's curative powers. There is, however, no lack of the saint's image, be it in sculpture, painting, or in stained glass, and the empty tomb beside the mysterious stone also has a reposing effigy of Fiachra on it. His relics were removed to the cathedral of Meaux for safety during the 16th-century Calvinist disturbances. In the former abbey grounds of Breuil the west wall of a 17th-century refectory can be seen. Beyond the tended garden lawns is the site of Fiachra's hospice, with the building that replaced it. Fittingly, in the 19th century, it served as an orphanage.

About a mile from the village of Montceaux to the north lies Saint Fiachra's holy well, with a small chapel erected in 1852. Over the door is the inscription: *Divio Fiacrio Anachorete*. Inside stands a statue of the saint. Called locally 'l'Ermitage', this chapel is supposed to supersede the *desertum*. The well beside it is still visited for cures.

Although the cult of Saint Fiachra is widespread in France – the see of Meaux alone having twelve churches or chapels answering to his name – few possess relics. Meaux cathedral was devastated so shockingly in the wars of the 16th century that not even an image of our saint survived. He now has again his chapel to the right of the high altar, with a stained-glass window depicting his miraculous feats – a donation the people made to their bishop in 1927 (plate 16).

History has recorded many later anecdotes regarding the cult, that illustrate Fiachra's popularity and the efficacy of cures sought for and granted in his name. These cover a wide range of ailments and involve many notabilities, cardinals, kings and consorts travelling to his shrine. The French queen Anne d'Autriche betook herself to Breuil barefoot on a public pilgrimage, where she dutifully declined to cross the threshold of the church. Twice an English king tried to steal the relics. Henry V was prevented from doing so by his fiery steed refusing to jump the trench. Edward the Black Prince got away with them as far as Normandy, it is said, where, having deposited them overnight in a church, he found them next morning glued to the altar!

Tourists in far-off Vienna may take a tour of the Austrian capital in a quaint black horse-drawn cab called a *Fiaker*, a fiacre. The coachman will gladly tell them a yarn about 'Sankt Fiaker' shipping over from Ireland in just such a vehicle. In truth, the cab originated in Paris, where in the 17th century indulgences were granted by the bishop of Meaux to pilgrims visiting the shrine of Saint Fiachra in his cathedral. An enterprising innkeeper in the Faubourg Saint-Antoine struck on the idea of organizing a cab service for transporting Parisians to Meaux. His establishment, the embarking point for pilgrimages, served by a team of 'cochers de Fiacre' became the Hôtel Saint-Fiacre, with the saint's effigy over the door. And so the coachman's estimable vocation developed into a corporation of taxi-drivers, a worldwide body that enjoys the patronage of Saint Fiachra – who probably hailed from Kilkenny!

Twenty kilometres further up the Marne valley from Meaux, the square-towered Benedictine abbey of Notre-Dame-de-Jouarre greets us from a rise. One of the oldest and most distinguished convents of France, Jouarre was first a double monastery, founded around the year 630 and following, in a slightly modified form, the precepts of Luxeuil.

Of its three original abbey churches the massive tower is all that remains. But Jouarre can boast of possessing one of the most famous Merovingian crypts in existence, the 7th-century *Crypte Saint-Paul* (plate 3). Entering it, we discover the tombs of the founder abbot Ado, of early bishops of Paris and Meaux who were connected with Jouarre, as well as that of its first abbesses. Among these, awaiting the Day of Judgement, lies a lovely lady, represented in stone on her sarcophagus with a dog at her feet, a book on her breast, and a crown of trefoil design in her hair. This is the 7th century Sainte Osanne, who is recorded as being the daughter of an Irish king, *fille d'un roi Scot*. If so, her name could be Osnait.

Tradition recalls Osanne's arrival on the 'Sacred Hill of Jouarre', drawn by a team of oxen – nothing unusual in those days for royalty, and probably implying an ancient rite. Here in Jouarre, where Osanne's foot first touched the ground, a spring appeared. This is the abbey's legendary holy well, 'La sain(t)e fontaine', its water qualified as the purest and sweetest in the region.

The institution of the abbey of Notre-Dame-de-Jouarre illustrates

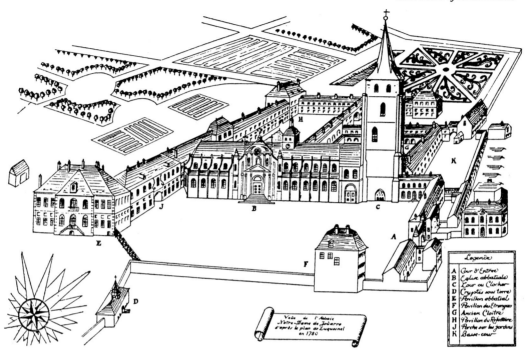

Legende

A   Cour d'Entrée
B   Eglise abbatiale
C   Tour ou Clocher
D   Cryptes sous terre
E   Pavillon abbatial
F   Pavillon des Etrangers
G   Ancien Cloître
H   Pavillon du Réfectoire
J   Porche sur les jardins
K   Basse-cour

Vue de l'Abbaie
Notre-Dame de Jouarre
d'après le plan de Luquesnel
en 1780

Plan of the abbey of Notre-Dame-de-Jouarre, by Duquesnil, 1780. The crypt of St Paul is marked D (lower left).

Ireland's strong continental ties with Merovingian France, concentrating in the tributaries of the Seine. Reaching its peak in the 7th century, a chain of monastic foundations arose, connected with Luxeuil and initiated by the personal contact Columban had with the region. For it was here, in close proximity to Meaux, that the Irish missionary stopped in 610 and blessed the children of local nobles whose hospitality he enjoyed. These children were later to become Columban's most ardent followers – Faro, whom we met in connection with Fiachra, his sister Fara, who founded the abbey of Faremoutiers in 617, as well as the three brothers Ado, Rado, and Ouen (Saint Audoen, whose cult the Normans were to bring to Dublin). These brothers assisted each other in instituting Jouarre, Rebais and Reuil, all in the vicinity and all modelled on Columban's Luxeuil.

Privileged in every respect and greatly endowed, these royal abbeys were patronized by the Franconian aristocracy as seats of learning. There inmates soon included the nobility of England, where, at that time, the church suffered a backlash and, as Bede tells his readers, monasteries were scarce. Perhaps these cross-channel arrivals were in

50

accordance with Pope Gregory's instructions of 595. The policy was to purchase Anglo–Saxon slaves, re-educate them, and send them back as Christian missionaries to England.

Here one might argue that slaves were not aristocrats. But then, Bathilde, the wife of Clovis II, was a former Anglo–Saxon slave. It was she who organized the introduction of English novices into French convents north of the Loire. These houses, such as Corbie on the Somme, took their guidance from Luxeuil, and it was from Luxeuil, at the queen's wish, that they were stocked. Chelles Abbey on the Marne was affiliated to Jouarre, which supplied it with inmates and at least one abbess (its first).

We mention these Anglian connections because, due to them, it has since been suggested that Osanne was not Irish but the daughter of a Northumbrian king who died in 716.

There is, however, nothing to sustain the hypothesis, apart from the fact that the renowned 7th-century bishop of Paris, Agilbert, who is

St Osanne in the crypt of St Paul, Jouarre.

12th-century tower (since restored) of Jouarre abbey.

buried in Jouarre where he began his career as a monk, had been for a short period bishop of Dorchester in England. But Agilbert's Irish connections need to be taken into account also, for his part in the Anglo-Saxon mission had been proceeded by years of study in Ireland. Agilbert's beautifully decorated sarcophagus in the crypt of Jouarre abbey is beside that of his sister Theodechilde, the first abbess.

As nothing further is known about Osanne, some hagiologists have also confused her with Osmanna, a recluse of Saint-Brieuc in Brittany, reportedly also of Irish origin. The fire that ravaged the abbey of Jouarre in the 15th century in the throes of the Hundred Years' War destroyed its historical documents that were kept in the tower. And so we are left with this 'daughter of an Irish king' behind her veil of mystery. After having slumbered in a modest grave for over five hundred years, she was suddenly accorded the honour of a *translatio*. The reason for this and for the strikingly elegant sepulchre she was accorded in the crypt of Saint-Paul in Jouarre, was probably the intervention of Saint Louis, the French king who was devoted to Saint Fursa. He would have been well aware of the documentary evidence concerning Osanne, then kept in the tower. Louis's victory over the English invaders in the year 1243 may have prompted the king of France to make this gesture — a tribute to Ireland, still in captivity. And this association leads us downstream from Jouarre to the site of Saint Fursa's abbey on the Marne.

It is difficult for us today to envisage the curving wooded valley of the stream through which the Vikings thrust their way; now the seat of industry and commerce where hardly a tree can breathe, and invaded by those later barbarians Mickey Mouse and his consorts (Eurodisneyland). This agglomeration of human design, officially titled 'Marne-La-Vallée', includes the Lagny of old, Fursa's 7th-century monastery of 'Sancta Petri de Latiniaco' on the river slope, and the walled-in town that developed around the royal abbey, long famed for its fairs, with barges coming up from as far as Paris to attend them.

The Benedictine block we meet there, presiding in the heart of the old town and now serving the magistrate, is the medieval successor of Fursa's foundation, granted him and built for him by Erchinoald, royal steward at the palace of the Merovingian king Clovis II in the year 648

52

— as a plaque on the wall reminds us — and destroyed by the Norsemen in the 9th century. At its inception put under the patronage of Saint Peter, the institution has remained so, as Fursa wished, down to our day, when in 1950 the title of 'Notre-Dames-des-Ardents' was added to it. We are referring to Lagny's present parish church, formerly that of the abbey, the only one to survive the French Revolution, that took over parochial duties for the citizens in 1792, when all the abbey's other parishes where suppressed.

The church of one of Lagny's former parishes is also known to have been founded by Fursa. Rebuilt after the Viking raids, it was henceforth called after him: Saint-Furcy (Fursy). When viewing the surviving Gothic façade, after the church's demolition in the throes of the French Revolution, we can estimate its grandeur. Now happily repaired, it stands facing the Place de la Fontaine, graced with Fursa's restored holy well. Here bonfires were lit on the patron's feastday in January, when the water was blessed — a reminder of the miraculous feat attributed to Saint Fursa, who provided his abbey with water from an underground spring. This deep source, in a vaulted chamber and canalized in the Middle Ages, is under the rue du Dr Naudier and can be visited at one's own risk. Having served the town for centuries as its one-and-only supply of drinking-water, from which surrounding lands also benefited,

53

Subterranean source of St Fursa, Lagny. Sketch by Cavallo-Peduzzi, 1907.

it suddenly lost quality and quantity during the French Revolution(!). The legend attached to the spring is echoed in a stained-glass window signed by Claude Lévêque in 1883, one of several panels in the choir showing Fursa as a worker of miracles.

The church we enter into today was planned in the 13th century, when the abbey was in its prime. It never attained the dimensions intended, but is limited to the transept and (lowered) choir. Religious wars, foreign invasions and revolutions killed Lagny's aspirations, reducing the town to a state of lethargy and dilapidation, its abbey robbed and desecrated. In the 19th century the municipality remembering its ancient heritage re-purchased the monastery complex and proceeded to restore the core of Lagny.

Irretrievable were the abbey's objects of art such as the patron saint's bust-reliquary, melted down in the French Revolution. Its contents, part of Fursa's cranium, were salvaged and are now kept in the church in a bronze, neo-Gothic reliquary dating from 1902. For older shrines we have to look farther afield, there where they escaped notice, strewn around Picardy and Belgium, hidden often in village chapels. In the diocese of Amiens the cult of Saint Fursa has curiously enough always been stronger than in the vicinity of Lagny. Many wells are named after the saint whose healing powers, as with most Irish missionaries, are associated with water – produced by a stroke of his staff.

Fursa is quite the most remarkable Irishman to leave his mark on France in the wake of Columban. His influence exceeds that of Fiachra, for not only did he bring a group of trained missionaries with him, but he drew more highly competent men across the sea, whose ministry spread into lands north of the Somme, where pockets of paganism prevailed. Dates differ as to the arrival of Fursa. It may be in 641 that he was welcomed at the court of Clovis II, king of Neustria and Burgundy. Sailing from East Anglia, he had taken from his monastery of Cnobheresburg a party of pilgrims destined for Rome. Near the Somme estuary Fursa was greeted by duke Haimo of Ponthieu, who entertained him in his castle at Mézerolles. There the first miracle is recorded: Fursa heals his host's mortally stricken child. This, with other supernatural occurrences, is brought to the attention of the said major-domo Erchinoald in the citadel of Péronne. He invites Fursa to the capital with the prospect of a new church. Declining to stay before

LES SAINTS DE LAGNY

Saint Fursy *fondateur du Monastère de LAGNY (648). Mort en 650*

Saint Emilien *Successeur de Saint Fursy, acheva la Construction du Monastère*

Saint Eloque *Troisième Abbé de LAGNY, reçut à Péronne le dernier soupir de Saint Fursy*

Saint Momble *Ordonné prêtre par St ELOI, fondateur de Villemomble; Mort en 665*

Saint Kentigern *Un des premiers moines de LAGNY, compagnon des Courses Apostoliques de St Fursy.*

Saint Algis *Disciple de Saint Fursy   Mort en 670.* **Sts ETHON** *et* **COLEBAN**

Saint Deodat *Moine de LAGNY, Chorévêque de PARIS, inhumé dans l'église abbatiale*

Saint Maldegaire *Renonce au monde. Devient religieux de LAGNY, fonde les Monastères de ——— Haumont et de Soignies.*

Saint Landry *Fils de Maldegaire, devient évêque de Meaux — Mort en 675*

Saint Fulbert, Saint Ausilion, Saint Sidoine, *Religieux de l'Abbaye de LAGNY, leurs tombeaux furent détruits par les Normands au IXe Siècle*

Sainte Jeanne d'Arc, *accomplit à LAGNY l'unique miracle visible de sa Vie.*

having completed his Rome pilgrimage, the Irishman moves on. Returning to Péronne, as promised, he is offered means for establishing a monastery in the Marne valley where, in the 4th century, a Roman colonist called Latinius had left his name on a hill site (hence 'Lagny').

Erchinoald, in the meantime, proceeded to build the collegiate church in Péronne, to replace the chapel of Mont-des-Cygnes, where Fursa had already deposited relics of Saint Patrick and other Irish saints. Erchinoald also set about establishing another church in the neighbouring Mont-Saint-Quentin for his guests. The first abbot here was to be Fursa's brother Ultán.

In Lagny Fursa builds beside his priory a hospital, the precursor of the present one, in which its patron is portrayed in a modern stained-

Plaque in Lagny's parish church commemorating Irish saints — and Joan of Arc!

55

View of Péronne, by Matthäus Merian, 1655, with prominence given to the church of St-Furcy (centre).

glass window. Just inside the parish church a plaque commemorates 'Les Saints de Lagny', where the names are engraved of Fursa's companions and disciples who laboured here and whose tombs were destroyed by the Vikings. One of Lévêque's window panes portrays the translation of the saint's shrine to Péronne in the 13th century, where a new abbey was erected over the ruins of the first Irish one – the Chapitre Royal de Saint-Fursy. This, together with the gift of a precious shrine, was an act of thanksgiving for the safe return of the French king Louis IX – the Saint Louis of history – from the crusade of 1256, attributed to the intercession of Saint Fursa. Veneration of the Irish saint was then at a new height, when great attention was paid to his famous gift of prophesy. Monks were busy transcribing Fursa's visionary description of hell, *Fís Fhursa ar Ifreann*, a work that enjoyed popularity in the Christian world long before Dante's *Inferno*.

The French king's gesture in transferring the relics to Péronne is comprehensible in view of the losses inflicted on that ancient Merovingian seat through wars and invasions. Part of Péronne's citadel wall is preserved, beside which lies the holy well of Saint Fursy, much frequented in former times. The pilgrim's path leading to it has since become a street bearing the saint's name. Local archives have frequent reference to the lively cult of the patron saint, for throughout its turbulent history Péronne clung to his protection. The famous siege of the city in the year 1536, with its 'miraculous delivery due to Saint Fursy', was commemorated ever after with a procession in his honour, carrying a banner with his painted silk and embroidered effigy. This cherished object, kept in the City Hall, disappeared in World War I. But many drawings were made of 'La bannière du siège de Péronne', and these are exhibited in the town museum.

Its chapter dissolved in the French Revolution, Péronne's famous abbey of Saint-Fursy was sold and then demolished. Part of the site is taken up today by the Palais de Justice. All that had been salvaged of the church contents was brought to the church of Saint John Baptist – only to suffer there further desecration. But Fursa still has his altar, where his salvaged wooden statue is flanked with those of his two brothers, Ultán and Faolán, abbots in Péronne after him. Predominant in Fursa's iconography, here as elsewhere, are the oxen at his feet. According to tradition, Fursa died in Mézerolles, after having left Lagny in the care of his fellow missionaries. Promptly, both the duke

56

of Ponthieu and the major-domo Erchinoald claimed his body for burial. To solve the matter peacefully, a pair of oxen was attached to the bier with the saint's remains and sent wandering off at will. The team took the road to Péronne.

Erchinoald made sure that his precious acquisition would reach the capital of Neustria safely, by force, if necessary, by sending a mounted guard down the road to meet the convoy. They met in a place north-east of Péronne, since called Lesboeufs(!), which has in its church a beautiful oil painting of Fursa, its patron saint.

Erchinoald's new church was the pride of Péronne. Fursa's uncorrupted remains drew the crowds, as stories of marvels and cures spread. Many Irish pilgrims stopped here to pray at his tomb on their way to Rome. Soon the city was known as *Peronna Scottorum* (Péronne of the Irish), styled by the scribes of Ireland *Cathair Fhursa*. The college of

Missal (1855) from Péronne. Frontispiece taken from the 17th-century engraving of St Fursa by J. Faros.

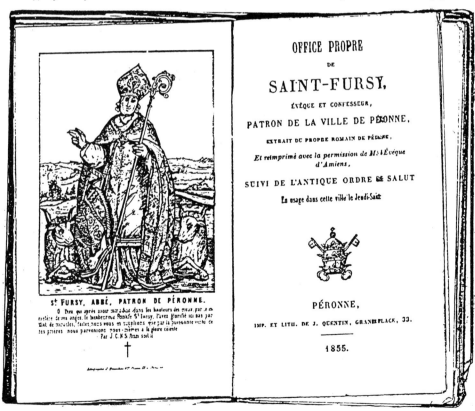

Silver shrine, 14th-century, from Gueschart, Somme. The oxen are portrayed drawing St Fursa's remains to Péronne.

Saint Fursa, in the hands of his followers, became a proud seat of Christian learning, providing education for the leading families of France. Above all else, it embodied the missionary spirit of its patron, with an apostolate that spread northward into heathen backwaters of old *Gallia Belgica*.

For centuries Mézerolles clung to the memory of Fursa, and a vivid cult spread through Ponthieu. Where duke Haimo had his fortress stands the grand château of Remaisil, beside which Frohens-le-Grand and Frohens-le-Petit bear the saint's name in a contorted form. 'Frohens' derives from the Flemish *Furs-hem*, the abode of Fursa. Both villages have sanctuaries dedicated to Fursa, and between them and Mézerolles is La Fontaine, where the resuscitation of the duke's child was believed to have taken place. And if cobwebs in the windows of Chapelle Saint-Fursy denote the fading of man's memory, the pious *hommage* inscribed over the door of the chapel in Frohens-le-Grand may one day re-awaken it!

The Somme valley and the plateau of Picardy is a stretch of land studded with the imprints of early Irish evangelists, but space does not permit us to mention them all. Passing Amiens, where we can admire our 5th-century bishop German in the Musée de Picardie, in a 16th-century stained-glass window from the church of Saint-Germain-l'Écossais, we take a road to the south-west leading to that martyr's burial place already alluded to, St-Germain-sur-Bresle. A church portrait confronts us there with the legend: the patron saint in the process of thrusting the horrific seven-headed dragon down a well. German's statue also decorates the entrance to the church of Saint Vulfran in Abbeville; but between Amiens and Abbeville we should not fail to take time out for the grandiose Saint-Riquier, of France's many Gothic churches one of the noblest, and steeped in Irish memories.

Saint-Riquier supersedes that of an abbey of great renown – Centula, the present monastery of which houses a museum. Many relics of early Irish evangelists were gathered and stored in the church of Saint-Riquier, among them those of Columban, Fursa, and Ponthieu's revered hermit-saint Maugille (Maldegaire, Madelgisel), a member of Fursa's group in Lagny who, accompanying him on his last journey, remained and laboured in the land between the Somme and Authie estuaries after Fursa's demise. Considered most precious of all were the relics of Caidoc and Fricor (Adrien), the two Irish monks who in the early 7th century converted the local lord Riquier (Raichar, Richarius). This nobleman gave his slaves freedom, renounced title and riches and built a monastery on his estate in which he then took orders – those of Columban. Saint Riquier is portrayed at the church entrance among other Gothic effigies, including a (mutilated) Fursa.

Originally following the Rule of Columban, Centula changed to that of Saint Benedict and, expanding in 790 to hold 400 inmates, played an influential rôle in the Carolingian Renaissance, its abbot Angilbert being secretly wed to Charlemagne's daughter! Richly endowed, Centula's famous codex (illuminated Gospels), dating from before Charlemagne's coronation in 800, is now kept in Abbeville's municipal library and is on view.

All considered, there is nowhere in continental Europe where Irish missionaries of the period ploughed the field more intensely than in this corner of France, and there is much about them still to be unravelled. Quentowic and other cross-channel ports made this quiet invasion possible; the *peregrini*, mainly on foot, working their way up the various streams inland. And again, this would not have borne fruit as it did, but for the protection, the moral engagement and the generosity of those much maligned Franconian rulers. A story, brief and touching, has come down to us about a bestowal of land on the Irish. It concerns Fursa and this is the Irish version as documented in the monastery of Tallaght:

> She [of unnamed nobility] said to Fursa: 'What manner of a person art thou?'
> 'I am like an old smith with his anvil on his back,' said Fursa.
> 'If God were to give thee a block on which to place the anvil, wouldst thou there abide?' said she.
> 'That would indeed be likely,' he said. Whereupon she bestowed on him the place where he was.

The narrative suggests that the sponsor – probably Saint Gertrud of Nivelles – was dealing with a fatigued elderly craftsman, as indeed was the case. Fursa had a long and distinguished career behind him on reaching France, and is reputed to have been a skilled metalworker. Fursa's steps lead back from the Paris Basin and Picardy to East Anglia (where he became patron of the see of Northampton) and from there back to County Louth, where he was long remembered as

St-Riquier. Detail of the Gothic façade.

*Frohens-le-Grand. Chapel
dedicated to St Fursa.*

*Frohens-le-Petit. Cemetery
and 'chapelle Saint-Furcy'.*

'Saint Purce' of the monastery of Saint Mochta. He also has his place in the topography of County Galway, from where he probably hailed, being christened on the banks of the Corrib by his uncle Saint Brendan and educated in the island monastery of *Inis Moccu Cuinn*. From there – to quote Bede – he took relics of local saints that he deposited in Péronne along with those of Saint Patrick, whose cult he obviously came into contact with during his sojourn in Louth in the diocese of Armagh.

It is thought to be Fursa, then, who introduced the cult of Saint Patrick into northern France. Péronne 'of the Irish', the capital of Merovingian Neustria in those troubled days, is the kernel of the French nation we know.

Fursa had left his younger brothers Ultán and Faolán in charge of his English monastery at Cnobheresburg. This establishment had been founded under the auspices of the Anglo-Saxon king Sigisbert who, when exiled in Gaul had come into contact with Columban's teaching in Burgundy, from where, at his wish on returning, a certain bishop Felix came to shoulder the work of evangelization in East Anglia along with the Irish. But it was not long before the joint venture was in jeopardy. Sigisbert was slain and his army massacred by Penda, the pagan king of Mercia; a turn of events that brought the Anglo-Saxon mission to an abrupt end. Taking with them all the books they could carry, the Irish monks fled to the Continent, where their missionary training found appreciation and was speedily put to the test. Following Fursa's footsteps, their field of activity soon widened to include the Low Countries, Brabant, Artois and Flanders. They preached in the valleys of the Sambre and Meuse, from where they penetrated into wilder parts, such as the Ardennes forest range.

The disciples who had accompanied Fursa did not stray that far. Several were allotted the monastery of Saint-Vincent in Laon as a headquarters to operate from, among them Boetien, already mentioned in connection with that diocese. But the one who represents this group best is the martyr Gobán (listed in Lagny as 'Coleban'). He left a deep imprint on folk memory, and on the topography of what is now the Département of Aisne in Picardy, as 'Saint Gobain', and we have no trouble tracing him.

The fastness of 'Laon Clavato' (the enclosed), as it was known of old, failed to satisfy Gobán or give him the scope necessary for what he considered his calling. At his request king Clovis then granted him land

ECCLESIAR·AB·ANGILBERTO·APVD·CENTVLAM·AN·DCC·XCIX
CONSTRVCTARVM·E·SCRIPTO·CODICE·____·EKMATEION

Centula. The royal abbey of St Richarius. Engraving of 1612, copied from a drawing in the Cronicon Centulense (1088).

Parish church of Saint-Gobain, on Mont Erème, Aisne.

for a hermitage in the vast primeval forest to the west of Laon (of this, 6000 hectares remain, called 'La forêt de Saint Gobain' and under preservation). After crossing its deep ravines, Gobán climbed a height where he fell asleep, and on awakening, at the prod of his staff, a spring appeared. Here he decided to settle, building himself a cell and an oratory that he dedicated to Saint Peter.

After years of labour in his forest glade, Gobán was murdered in his oratory in the year 670. Vandals roaming the land were responsible, the natives insisted. There where they found him, they buried him with great mourning, on the slope of the hill.

This came to be known as 'Mont Erème', the hermit's mound, or 'Mont du Desert'; a great pilgrim resort. The spring was said to have curative powers, and miracles were recorded at the martyr's tomb in the chapel, tended by the Benedictines of Saint Vincent's. In 1068 a priory was built, affiliated to the monastery in Laon, and around the

'Les rochers de l'Ermitage', site in the forest of Saint-Gobain.

new pilgrim's church a cluster of houses appeared – the hamlet of Saint-Gobain. The stately parochial church we find there today had many predecessors, what with the ravages of warring generations finding their way somehow through the huge forest to the clearing. What they did not discover was the remarkably large vaulted subterranean sanctuary beneath the church, which is well worth a visit. It contains the spring and original grave of its founder, whose relics are now in the church above. An old statue of Gobán, badly mutilated in the French Revolution and removed from its niche beside the church entrance, is also in the crypt. Another effigy that stood outside the church with a stone at its base called 'the hermit's pillow' has since disappeared. The patron's feastday is celebrated in Saint-Gobain, and in the dioceses of Laon, Soissons and Saint-Quentin a special collect is read.

Gobán's iconography presents an elderly, bearded man holding either a book, or the palm of martyrdom, grasping his Irish *cambutta*, that took him so far, through a span of life that reached from the West of Ireland to County Louth, and over to East Anglia and on to France with Fursa, for, like his master, Gobán was a Galwegian.

Well marked walks through the beautiful forest of Saint-Gobain will lead us to a group of boulders called 'Les rochers de l'Ermitage'. Nearby a heap of stones are still revered as Gobán's cell where, like all true anchorites, he gathered strength in solitude and prayer.

BELGIUM AND HOLLAND

Passing on from Péronne into Belgium, we reach another important centre of Irish monasticism in 7th-century France. This is Nivelles, a town on an incline of the Thines valley. Founded by Itta, widow of the West Franconian major-domo Pippin I (Pippin von Landen), it was stocked with Irish monks from the start. Nivelles was to become one of the most prestigious of the many royal abbeys of the following Ottonian Empire. Its magnificent medieval façade, severely battered in World War II, has been faithfully restored and cannot fail to impress.

On the death of her husband in 640 Itta took the advice of bishop

Amandus – an Aquitanian like herself – in initiating a double monastery in Nivelles, modelled on that of Kildare. Saint Amandus was a trainee of the South, and first and foremost in the introduction of the precepts of Columban into newly formed bishoprics in the North. Called the 'Apostle of Flanders', he is mainly responsible for the settlements of Luxovian monks in Belgium. But if Itta was its first abbess, and Luxeuil its initial inspiration, Nivelles' prestige was attained under the guidance of Fursa's missionary party, and it is Itta's daughter Gertrud whose name is forever bound to Nivelles.

Shortly after Fursa's death in Mézerolles, Itta died, and for another decade Gertrud ruled the abbey until her own demise in 659. Her sister Begga headed the affiliated convent of Andenne on the river Meuse, filled with inmates from Nivelles. Likewise stocked and orientated were the abbeys of Lobbes and Aulne on the upper Sambre, founded by Landelin of Luxeuil. Unlike his namesake of the Rhineland, claimed to be Irish, this Landelin has no such pretensions – as far as we know. But hailing from Luxeuil with a name that has an Irish flavour, the question may be left open to doubt. His abbeys have gone, but Lobbes' pre-Romanesque church has survived and, with Aulne's great Cistercian abbey ruins of 1147, stands to remind us of their forceful Columban origin.

A curious discovery was made during the restoration of the great collegiate church in Nivelles. Probing into its Merovingian foundations, the original sepulchral crypt of Saint Gertrud's church came to light, and within it a tomb containing three skulls. It was then recalled that mention is made of Saint Faolán's three Irish companions, slain with him in the forest nearby, and that they were also brought to Nivelles for burial. The site under the church aisle is open to the public. And this turns our attention to Faolán and Ultán, brothers of Fursa.

Coming from Fursa's missionary centre in East Anglia, it was naturally their lot to follow his footsteps in France. Received at the Merovingian court around the year 649, they were soon installed in Péronne, which flourished under their leadership, Ultán taking over the adjacent Saint-Quentin as well. A hospice was attached to the Péronne monastery to cater for pilgrims arriving in ever greater numbers after Fursa's demise and wishing to pray at his tomb on their way to Rome. And so *Peronna Scottorum* remained, probably under the guidance of Irish abbots, until its destruction in 880.

Collegiate church of Ste-Gertrude, Nivelles.

Ruins of the Cistercian abbey, Aulne.

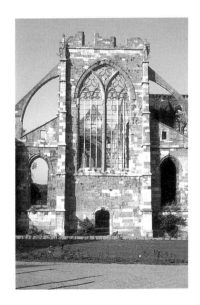

Statue of St Faolan, 18th-century, Fosses-la-Ville.

Fosses, as seen by Remacle Le Loup (18th-century). The church of St Brigid extra muros (far right).

The same fate awaited Nivelles, to which Faolán had resorted. This royal abbey, too, rose in importance after the death of its Irish bishop in 655.

Faolán had courted disaster in the same way as Gobán and others did. His ambition being to conquer new ground, he had not been content to stay in Nivelles. Pushing ahead, he reached the ruins of the Gallo-Roman *Vosseunis*, between the rivers Sambre and Meuse, and there, with the backing of his noble benefactors, in the year 635 he founded a monastery which he put under the patronage of Saint Brigid of Kildare – the royal abbey of Fosses.

In the 9th century, after heavy onslaughts from Norse invaders, Fosses still finds mention as a royal *monasterium scottorum*, showing that its spirit was rebounding and its abbey restored, enjoying now the patronage of the Carolingian dynasty. And in the 10th century, after new tribulations, this time caused by Hungarians, a generous donation permitted a larger church to be built to accommodate the concourse of pilgrims. Augustinian canons stayed here until suppressed by the French Revolution, the importance of the regal abbey having been greatly augmented by the transfer of its founder's martyred remains from Nivelles to Fosses in 1083. Many marvels were subsequently reported. Excavations carried out in the church in 1951–2 revealed massive pillars built under the choir to support the pilgrims' passage beneath, proceeding in U-form around the saint's tomb under the high

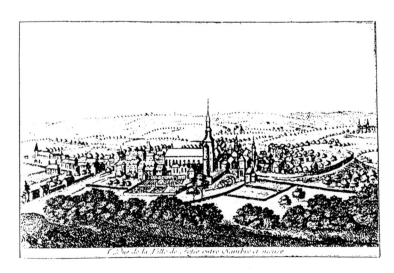

Tableau in the church choir, Fosses: the discovery of St Faolan's body by St Gertrud.

Entrance to the church of St-Feuillen, Fosses, with the patron's image over the door and the earlier Augustinian tower beyond.

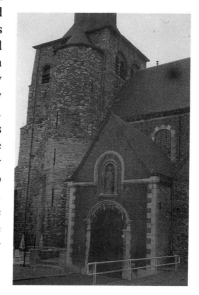

altar. This great cryptal chamber, together with the tower of the church are medieval, also the chancel, which displays carved stalls of 1524 and a series of large 18th-century oil paintings, portraying Saint Faolán's life and death. The saint's reliquaries in a costly silver bust are carried every seven years around the former monastic territory in a procession called 'La Marche de Saint Feuillen'. Most pronounced is the military element of this colourful pageant. It reflects the dangers incurred by transporting these treasures through woods and uninhabited grounds. An armed guard was formed for protection against robbers, and this became ritual. Now the whole parish turns up in uniform, mostly of the Napoleonic period, with many on horseback, to celebrate Faolán's feastday in July. This entails a symbolic inspection of the abbatial domain – no longer extant – to receive an albeit posthumous consecration by its founder. The *marche* of the relics takes up a whole day, advancing under the blaze of fifes and drums. Stops are made at seven stations along the route, where shots are fired into the air. Of all the many rites and processions involving Irish saints, that of Fosses is surely the most spectacular (plate 14).

Faolán was returning to Fosses after visiting his brother Ultán for the

65

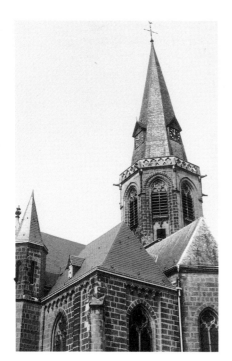

*Le Roeulx, church of
St-Feuillen.*

*Statues of Sts Faolan,
Gertrud (left) and Brigid
in the crypt, Fosses.*

feast of Saint Quentin when he fell into the hands of marauders in a wood near Le Roeulx. Tradition affirms that after a search of two months it was Saint Gertrud herself who discovered Faolán's incorrupt body. With a great display of pomp and mourning the bier was carried by the nobles back to Nivelles. Gertrud had a church built in Le Roeulx with a priory for Irish monks. This was later taken over by the Augustinian Premonstratensian order, who were thrown out in the course of the French Revolution. All we find in Le Roeulx today is a parish church with a side-altar dedicated to Saint Faolán. It also possesses a relic of the Irish martyr.

In Fosses itself there are many items to arrest our attention in what is

66

now the parish church of Saint-Feuillen. A tableau at the altar of Saint
Ultán depicts the legend of the bloodstained dove bringing news of
Faolán's murder to his brother in Saint-Quentin (a reminder of the
visionary gift Ultán shared with his brother Fursa). All three brothers
are shown in one of the tableaux in the choir, being christened in Ireland
by Saint Brendan. In the cryptal chamber behind the altar, old effigies
of Saint Brigid and Saint Gertrud guard the place where Faolán's remains
first reposed. And the particular devotion paid by the saint to his Irish
patron again bears evidence in a small church that tops a hill beside the
town, to which the rue Sainte-Brigitte leads us. Said to have been erected
by Faolán and his monks, it has a Celtic cross inserted in the outer wall of
the sanctuary, believed to have been the altar stone of the original 7th-
century church, brought hither from Ireland! Be that as it may, Faolán is
certainly responsible for implanting the very lively cult of Saint Brigid into
this part of Belgium – a cult still practised at this ancient place. People
gather here to celebrate her feast day, bringing twigs bound together to

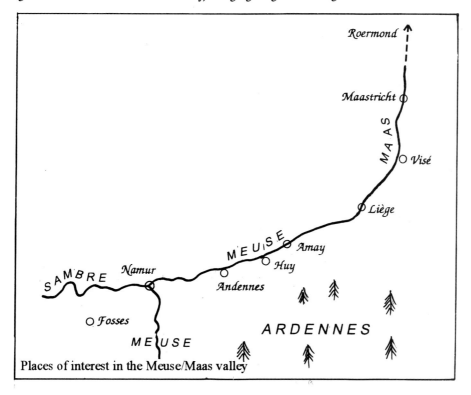

Places of interest in the Meuse/Maas valley

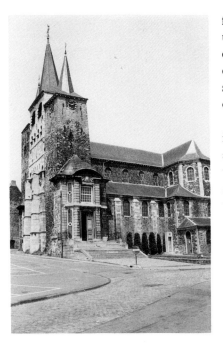

Amay. Collegiate church of Sts-Georges-et-Oda.

form a *cros Bríde*, as in Ireland. After being blessed, these crosses are hung up in cow-sheds to protect the cattle for another year. Also reminiscent of the charitable aspect of the cult of Saint Brigid is the large hospital-cum-old folk's home beside the church on the hill, superseding, it is said, the original almshouse of the Irish missionaries. The nuns in charge of the hospital also have the keys to the church of Sainte-Brigitte.

Devotion to Saint Faolán, fanning out in all directions from Fosses, is marked with churches and chapels in his honour. And since rivers are destined to be the carriers of man's history, it was the proximity of the river Meuse – Maas in Germanic tongues – that played the part of spreading Faolán's cult and reputation. A chain of citadels inherited by the Franks lay on its banks – Namur, once a Celto-Roman *oppidum*, Amay, and the ancient trade depot of Huy; Liège (Lüttich) and Maastricht, bishoprics of the early 7th century – settlements quick to respond to the story of the martyred founder of Fosses. A visitor of today can enjoy the gay pageantry that Liège stages in honour of 'Saint Pholien' in the month of June.

The Meuse valley's preoccupation with the cult of Faolán affected that of Saint Brigid. As a protectress of cattle her fame progressed through the land and across the river into the diocese of Cologne. An important Roman road linked *Gallia Belgica* with the Rhinelands via Maastricht, soon to be complemented by a Carolingian trade-route linking the North Sea port of Brugge with the seat of Charlemagne at Aachen (Aix) and on to Cologne, the famed 'City of Holy Martyrs' – where Saint Brigid of Ireland, although no martyr, installed herself with a parish of her own in the city's core.

In the cathedral of Aachen, Brigid shares a stained-glass window with Faolán, whose adjacent church, that had served the community since the 15th century, has been rebuilt after destruction in World War II. (The connection between Faolán and Brigid was carried as far as Spain, where their effigies adorn an early church in Navarre.)

In Amay on the Meuse the church of Saint Brigid with its cults, rites and processions is gone forever, but we find her statue on entering the stately basilica of the parish, Saints-Georges-et-Oda. There the main focus is on the patroness, Oda, who remains historically a controversial figure. Efforts to solve the question of her identity were renewed by the sensational discovery in 1977 of a sarcophagus under the church choir, bearing the inscription *Sancta Chrodoara*. Tradition notes several saintly women of the name of Oda, who were probably associated with a nunnery existing here before the date 634. What concerns us in the maze of conflicting traditions, is the fact that of the various Odas or Chrodoaras in question, one, if not two, appear to have hailed from Ireland.

Either in the year 718 or 721, the episcopal see was moved from Maastricht to Liège by Saint Hubert, then bishop of the diocese. He did so in respect for his predecessor Saint Lambert, who was murdered in Liège in 705. The fame of Saint Lambert was widespread, and when news of his martyrdom reached Ireland a stream of pilgrims set out to visit his grave in Liège. One of these pilgrims was a girl named Oda (Odbha?). Some accounts say Oda was blind from birth, others say she was stricken with blindness on reaching the Continent. Whatever the case, Oda was cured at the tomb of Saint Lambert, famous for its miracles. Oda decided to stay as a recluse and devote her life to thanksgiving, in prayer and charity. She was granted a place for a hermitage in Brabant, in what is now Dutch territory, and there she remained within the precincts of a nobleman's fort, dying in the year 726.

Statue of St Oda in the Martinskerk, Sint-Oedenrode.

Such is the legend attached to the little town of Sint-Oedenrode — *rode* meaning a forest glade — a cult bringing a trail of pilgrims to Brabant to visit Oda's grave. By the early 12th century it became necessary for the then lord, Arnulf Van Rode, to build a church able to hold the crowds seeking cures at the shrine of *Oda virginis rodensis*, the virgin saint his ancestors had granted protection. This 'Odakerk', tended to by a chapter of canons, brought growth and prosperity to Sint-Oedenrode. Often destroyed and rebuilt in the course of Brabant's tumultuous history, it became the parish church, and when last repaired after the French Revolution was rededicated. The 'Odakerk' is the 'Martinskerk' of today.

Despite the change, and the modernization of the church's interior carried out in 1915, Oda is well represented. Her relics are displayed in a gilded silver shrine. While a portrait of her, painted before the French Revolution, bears the inscription *'ex Scotia fulget Roda'*, stained-glass windows give us her life story to muse on. Iconography presents Oda as a lover of nature (the bird) and a teacher, mainly of children (the book). Outside, at the back of the old graveyard we find Saint Oda's Chapel. It replaces the oratory built over her grave and traditionally the site of her modest hermitage, where prayers were offered and cures were

69

The healing of Oda by St Lambert. Stained-glass window in the church of Sint-Oedenrode.

reported through the ages. In Sint-Oedenrode an asylum for women was instituted in her name, that flourished from the 14th century on. It now houses the local museum.

To return to Amay and the Sancta Chrodoara whose name is chiselled on the 7th-century sarcophagus in the parish church, the opinion of modern scholars is that she is not of Irish origin. But we cannot be sure. Her tomb, considered a masterpiece of Merovingian stone masonry, is richly ornamented with patterns of Celtic interlacing. It portrays her with a Tau-shaped staff, also represented in the iconography of Ireland.

Indubitable is the presence of the Irish Oda of Sint-Oedenrode in the vicinity of Amay. Her cure, received in Liège at the tomb of Saint Lambert, is mentioned in a reliable source, the *Vita Landiberti vetustissima*.

The Saint Lambertus cathedral of Liège has been pulled down, but the square on which it stood, the Place Saint-Lambert, has bared its Merovingian foundation, revealing where Oda visited the honoured martyr's tomb. Without asking our readers to delve any deeper into the Oda puzzle, it is worth stating, for those who are interested, that, whoever that holy person was, she is quoted to have been given the Christian name of Oda (Ode in modern French) by her parents because it means 'a laud in Greek, and in the Irish tongue humility'. The Irish for 'humility' is *umhal*, phonetically very near *Oude* (the name given her by the 14th-century chronicler Jean d'Outremeuse of Liège). Jean d'Outremeuse presents *Oude d'Amay* to us as the widow of a duke of Aquitaine, who was killed in battle near Poitiers. She then found refuge in Brabant at the court of Pippin, together with her nephew, the boy who became later Saint Hubert. What if this *Oude d'Amay* were the 7th-century 'Odba of Brabant' of the genealogy of Cenel Laogaire? Is there a connexion between Oude, Odba, and *umhal*? If so, it is unlikely that Aquitainian parents would choose for their daughter the Milesian name *Odhbha*, familiar to Ireland and her mythology alone. With that we will take leave of the enigmatic Chrodoara in her sarcophagus, protected by a glass covering, but for all to see, in the place where she has slumbered since the early Middle Ages – the majestic collegiate church of Amay-sur-Meuse.

With their repeated incursions across the lower Rhine valley, the pagan

70

Saxons disrupted whatever furtive attempts the Romans had made to introduce Christian civilization into the northern periphery of their empire. After the collapse of Roman rule, they represented a real danger to Merovingian Gaul. Outposts such as Xanten and Nimwegen, too weak for a a bishopric, had since crumbled, and the churches of Utrecht and Soest, installed by Dagobert I in the early 7th century, proved too isolated for the episcopal see of Cologne to manage, succumbing as they soon did, to Saxon and Frisian pressure. There was evidently great scope for pastoral work here in the Lowlands of the Meuse and Rhine valleys and the wooded stretch between Maastricht and Utrecht, where elks roamed and bears were hunted. The task was taken over by Aquitanian, Burgundian, and mobile Irish bishops and priests, combined with other religious ministrants. While the former group was occupied with the restoration and re-organization of the bishoprics, it was the mainly Irish *peregrini* who bore the brunt of evangelizing the natives. Many of them steeped in the traditions of Luxeuil, these lonely ascetics combed through the land with a missionary rigour that ever distinguished the Family of Columban, be they Irish-born or not.

In the Ardennes mountains two remarkable men, setting out together, have left their mark: Remacle and Hadelin. The bear in Remacle's iconography indicates the remoteness of the places they penetrated. Whether they were French or Irish is not clear, but it was Irish monasticism they represented. The people of the Ardennes passed it down that those who brought their ancestors the Faith were 'sons of Columban', and therefore were considered Irish. And here again it is Saint Gertrud and her kin who gave these 'wandering bishops' their footing, supplying them with stations to operate from. In 648–50, in agreement with king Sigibert III, Gertrud's brother (the powerful major-domo Grimoald) built for Remacle the double monastery of Stablo-Malmedy. Under his abbacy Stablo – now Stavelot – became the pivot of the conversion of the Ardennes district. There we find Remacle's costly sarcophagus, two metres long, a masterpiece of decorative art for which the Meuse valley is famed. This marvel of medieval workmanship compares with the shrine of Hadelin in Visé, where we find the two saints portrayed together in a row of panels illustrating the saint's life as recorded in legend. The reliquary was brought to Visé by the Augustinians of the abbey of Celles in the year 1338. It was in Celles that Hadelin died in 690, the abbey taking its name from the saint's

Designs on the sarcophagus of St Chrodoara (7th-century). Church of Sts-Georges-et-Oda, Amay.

St Hadelin. Statue in his abbey church, Celles.

71

*Parish church of
St-Monon, Nassogne.*

*Nassogne. The chapel and
covered well of St Mono.*

cella, or hermitage. A visitor to the region at the beginning of autumn can admire the shrine of Hadelin, when carried round Visé in procession on his feastday, 3 September. It has a length of one and a half metres.

There is another, earlier saint of the Ardennes, whose Irish identity remains unquestioned. He is Mono, the martyr of Nassogne, a legendary figure of the early 7th century, whose place in oral tradition was fixed long before a *vita* was compiled for him in the 11th century. This informs us that to Mono 'God assigned a place in the Ardennes forest, beside the bubbling spring Nassania.'

Here, by the fount of Celto-Roman cults our hermit settled, built an oratory and taught the Gospel, until the day when imprudent

72

1 *St Fridolin changes the course of the Rhine at Säckingen: baroque fresco on the ceiling of the minster.*

2 *The altar of St Trudpert's chapel, over the saint's well in Münstertal, Black Forest. Rebuilt and enriched in 1694–1710.*

3 The 7th-century crypt of St Paul, Jouarre abbey, northern France, with the tombs of its founders, first abbesses, and St Osanne, whose head in stone rests on a pillow (far centre).

4 The priceless bust-reliquary in St Landelin's pilgrim church in the Black Forest. The gilded silver bust, 63 cm high, was made in 1506 to encase the skull of Landelin, whose martyrdom is portrayed on the clasp of his regal gown, with springs gushing from under his severed head and limbs. The inscription around the base begins: Magno nobilium natu preclare viroru(m) regibus e Scotis qui generosus ades . . . *under which the legend is depicted on 20 embossed panels of great artistry, that form the reliquary's octagonal base.*

5 The martyrdom of St Dymphna and St Gerebern: detail of the oaken 'Dimpna-retable' (1515) in the Sint-Dimpnakerk, Geel, Flanders.

6 *St Goar, with a model of his church and his large key of hospitality, in a window of the collegiate church, St Goar, Rhineland.*

7 *St Wendalin the Pilgrim portrayed as such on his cenotaph in the basilica of St Wendel, Saarland (c.1400).*

8 *A 17th-century oil painting in the minster of Mittelzell, Reichenau, extolling the achievements of St Pirmin. The saint is seen here in a boat between his island monastery and the mainland, strewn with churches he founded, the water in between filled with expelled reptiles.*

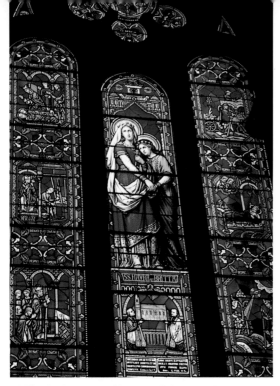

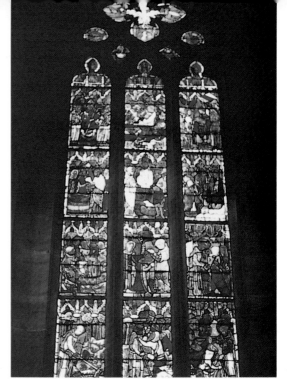

9 *The Irish martyrs Maure and Britta and their legend, illustrated in window panels in the church of Saint-Maure-de-Touraine.*

10 *The legend of St Florentius, the subject of one of the famous stained-glass windows of his church in Niederhaslach, Alsace.*

11 *Early 18th-century medallion showing the basilica of Sint Odilienberg with St Wiro (Maolmhuire), 'primo Geldriae apostolo', Holland.*

12 *On the shrine of the patron saints of Sint Odilienberg, Wiro, Plechelm and Otger are shown in relief receiving instructions from the pope in Rome.*

13 *The unveiling of the restored cross of St Efflam in the bay of Lannion, Brittany, 1993.*

14 *The 'Marche de Saint Feuillen', a tradition of the Belgium town of Fosses: the 1991 parade.*

15 *Local people assembling in 1993 at the well of St Wendalin, Saarland, for the annual blessing of farm vehicles and their horses (see plate 21).*

16 *Cardinal Ó Fiaich and other visitors from Armagh, at the cross in the bay of Guimorale, supposed landing-place of Columban in northern Brittany.*

17 *A priest of Meaux cathedral, France, holds a missal of 1709, showing the office for the feast of St Fiachra.*

18 *Schoolchildren of St-Fiacre-en-Brie, in the diocese of Meaux, with an image of their patron saint, assemble for the feastday celebrations, 1970.*

19 'La Grotte de Saint Colomban', the mountain retreat with the holy well, cave and (overbuilt with a chapel) stone bed of St Columban. Near Sainte-Marie-en-Chanois, Haute-Saône.

20 The festive 'Trudperti-Umgang' in Münstertal (Black Forest), 1989. To the left, the chapel of St Trudpert, built over the saint's well.

21 The pilgrimage site near St Wendel, Saarland: the chapel and hermitage that guard the well in the 'Valley of Wendalin'.

22 *Annegray. Remains of a Columban wall and the stump of a Roman pillar (Haute-Saône).*

23 *The basilica of St Wendel, Saarland.*

24 *Aerial view of the hilltop convent of Mont-Sainte-Odile, Alsace.*

criticism of a certain person's moral conduct brought his mission to an untimely end. Mono was slain in his cell at the spring of Nassania by a hired assassin, probably a woodcutter.

Informed of this, the bishop of Maastricht caused a sanctuary to be erected over the martyr's grave, and clerics were sent from Amay to offer Mass daily at the scene of the crime. Then in the 8th century, King Pippin the Small, impressed by the devotion of the forest dwellers to Mono's memory and their reports of posthumous healings, ordered a church to be built there with a chapterhouse for canons attached. To judge by its aftermath, Mono's apostolate must have been considerable.

To this day, celebrations are held in Nassogne on the first Sunday after Ascension, when a procession moves from the parish church of Saint-Monon to the chapel at the well of Nassiona – as the source Nassania is now called – where Mono's ancient sarcophagus lies. Reliquaries carried in the procession include the saint's staff, the iron remains of the axe with which he was killed, and his silver bell. This legendary Irish bell is said to have been unearthed by Mono's tamed boar – an occurrence often portrayed in his iconography. It may be taken to symbolize the ultimate triumph of Mono's creed, of light over darkness.

The little town of Nassogne, seated on its plateau in the depths of the Ardennes Forest confirms the amazing tenacity of folk memory. We have its people to thank for a picture of an Irish *peregrinus*, passed down in the liveliest of colours.

St Mono, above the altar in his chapel.

Roermond. The basilica on Sint Odilienberg (Mount St Peter).

Roermond, once an important seat on the lower Meuse – here called the Maas – has also had its share of political turmoil and devastations. Having passed through Austrian, Spanish and Belgian hands, the town now belongs to Holland – changes, that have not succeeded in eroding the memory of two Irish missionaries called 'the Apostles of the Guelderland', Wiro and Plechelm.

After having attended the synod of 697 in Rome, where they were made bishops by the pope, Wiro and Plechelm passed through this region on their return journey. Here Pippin II invited them to stay, offering land to settle on, that he would donate. And so, on a hill called after Saint Peter, they built a monastery, dedicating it to the Holy Virgin. During the founders' lifetime, king Pippin made yearly pilgrimages barefoot in Lent to this royal abbey he lavishly endowed.

73

Oldenzaal. Statue of St Plechelm beside his church.

Altar and shrine in St-Rumbout's cathedral in Mechelen.

In the 9th century the abbey on Mount Saint Peter was presented to the cathedral of Utrecht. Later on it was removed to Roermond, where it flourished under Augustinian rule. In spite of this, the majestic abbey church still crowns the hill, now re-christened Sint Odilienberg. It had suffered numerous pillages and demolitions before its last restoration as a parish church, when it was put under the patronage of the Cologne martyr Saint Odilia. After this, the cult of its founders waned. Since, however, Wiro's tomb was discovered in the excavations of 1881, pilgrimages to the shrines of the Irish apostles have been revived (plate 12).

The intrepidity of these Christian pioneers, wandering far out into the lower Rhine valley, can be judged by the many churches they founded in isolated regions. Their relics were honoured in various places, including Utrecht cathedral and the important chapter of Oldenzaal, where Plechelm's gilded shrine stands in his church.

A connection between this mission and that of Willibrord of Northumbria — setting out after twelve years of preparation in Ireland — is considered possible. Plechelm has sometimes been confounded with the Northumbrian Pecthelm, who is an entirely different person. The deacon Otger, who accompanied our two apostles on their travels, may have hailed from Northumbria, but names are no criterion. Wiro, who is claimed by County Clare, bears a name that is merely a distortion of the popular 'Maolmhuire' (plate 11).

Saint-Bavokathedraal in Gent, the capital of East Flanders, is the jealous guardian of Saint Livin's cloak. The saint referred to — immortalized by such famous painters as Rubens and Van Eyck — may, or may not be identical with our Irish Livin(n)ius, patron of Saint Levans in Cornwall. But Saint Rumold (Romaould, etc) has a stronger case to present. Patron of the archdiocese of Mechelen, this great apostle was for centuries so unanimously and vehemently called an Irishman, that we cannot lightly pass him by.

The tradition of Rumold's Irish heritage was strong enough for the 17th-century archbishop of Mechelen (Malines, Mecheln) to commission the Irish College in Louvain to provide a biography of the saint from gleanings from early sources. The scholars entrusted with the task were Aodh Mac a'Bhaird and Seán Mac Colgan who died before its completion. The work was then taken over by Tomás Ó Sírín. Up to that date, no account of the saint's life existed in writing, apart from the fabulous ramblings of a monk of Saint-Truiden, near Liège. Oral tradition called Rumold a 'stranger', a hermit, who after ministering to the people was eventually murdered near Liège. This would appear to have happened around the year 700. On Rumold's Irish provenance no doubt was ever cast.

Whatever the case, the remains of this hallowed 'stranger' are kept in a costly shrine in the cathedral of Mechelen, erected over the high altar between golden doors. A reminder of his fame is the mention made of him in the classical *Nibelungenlied*. And the citizens of Mechelen show their abiding attachment on the feastday of 'Saint Rombaut de Malines' with a great display of pomp (24 June).

Not far from Mechelen we come upon a townland of strange, if goodly, repute, upholding a custom that dates back to the 13th century. This entails the provision of private accommodation for visitors suffering from mental disorders. Such guests are welcomed unconditionally as pilgrims to the shrine of Saint Dimpna in the Flemish town of Geel.

Saint Dimpna, anglicized Dymphna, is by tradition an Irish person. Geel celebrates her as a virgin martyr who took refuge in the Low Countries, possibly as far back as the 6th century.

Canon Bourke, writing in the 19th century, tells us that in his time the feast of Saint Damhnait was celebrated in Cill Delga (Kildalkey) in the barony of Luighne, County Meath, on 15 May. This happens to be the feastday of Belgium's Sainte Dimpne, or Dimpna, patroness of Brabant. And the legend of Ireland's Damhnait is similar. A native of Oriel, she is the patron of Clogher, where she was born, and her church was *Tech Damnata*, 'the church of Damhnait'. There is a 'Tedavnet' place-name in Monaghan, and in County Cavan a ravine used to be shown, where Damhnait hid from her father's pursuing soldiers.

In Belgium, the relics of Saint Dymphna are carried every fifth year through the streets of Geel, a town that owes its existence to her, in a procession called in Flemish 'Sint-Dimpna-Omnegang'.

As patron saint of the insane, Dymphna has had charitable institutes established in her name as far apart as Austria and USA. All are modelled on the famous infirmary of Geel, the origin of which was a hospital, founded in the 13th century in connexion with the discovery of the saint's remains, together with those of her companion. This

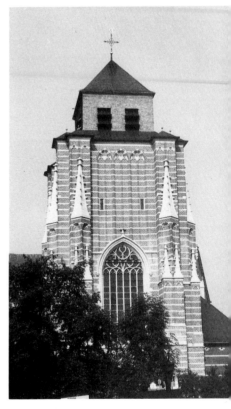

St-Dimpnakerk, Geel.

St Dymphna and her wicked Irish father. Late 19th-century stained-glass window in Geel church.

discovery confirmed the story passed down for generations regarding an Irish princess, killed in the forest of Geel along with her confessor, the priest Gerebern, by her 'possessed' father. Natives, it was told, had lain their bodies to rest in two Roman sarcophagi, to preserve them from wild beasts of the forest.

In one of the fragmented tombs, discovered in the 13th century, was a sheet of slate with the inscription *DIPH // NA*. The Carolingian-style lettering implied that the slate had been introduced into the sarcophagus at a later date. It became customary in Geel to attach this slate to the neck of a person afflicted with a nervous disease – epileptics, and others considered 'possessed' of an evil spirit. After the *translatio* of the relics, the cult of the supplicants took on such proportions that a hospital had to be erected for them in Geel.

Owing to the miraculous reputation of these relics, efforts were made to steal them by pilgrims from the Lower Rhine. They succeeded only in getting away with those of Gerebern. Deposited in the church

76

of Sonsbeck, near Xanten, they were invoked for complaints of fever and gout. But the fortune of Sonsbeck was shortlived. The 'Holy Robbers of Xanten', as they came to be known, were forced to restore Saint Gerebernus to his rightful place beside Saint Dymphna – a great day for the people of Geel, as we can well appreciate on viewing the picture commemorating it, on one of the oak panels of the famous altar-piece in the St-Dimpnakerk of Geel.

What, we might well ask, is at the back of all this? Early records failing, are we to depend entirely on rumours? No kind of documentation concerning Dymphna is available before around 1240, when an Augustinian monk of Cambrai, a certain Petrus Camarensis, offered a compilation of oral traditions, then at his disposal. This was made at the request of bishop Guido of Cambrai, whose concern was that Geel's popular patron saint, having occupied the minds and the lives of his flock for so long, should have a better foot to stand on, now that her relics were found.

This is Dymphna's story: Daughter of a pagan Irish king, whose wife had been converted by the cleric Gerebern, Dymphna was secretly christened at birth. On the death of his wife, the king searched Ireland for a woman to take her place, but could find no one to equal her in beauty – excepting their daughter Dymphna. In the heart of the king the devilish plan ripened, that he would marry his own daughter. At this infamous proposition Dymphna, together with the priest Gerebern, flees the country, taking with them the court jester and his wife. Landing at the port of Antwerp, they seek cover in the thickly forested region of Kampen. In a deserted chapel dedicated to Saint Martin near the village of Zammel they take refuge, and there they decide to remain and live the life of recluses.

Back in Ireland the king has not given up his evil intentions. He decides to bring Dymphna home by force. Taking a troop of soldiers with him, he sails across to northern Gaul. There the soldiers comb the wooded coast in vain, until the day when, tired and thirsty, they enter a tavern in the hamlet of Westerlo. Paying for refreshments in Irish coinage, the innkeeper's wife exclaims, that she has lately seen the like, receiving it from the hands of strangers.

Thus the hideout of Dymphna is revealed. She is brought to the place where the king is waiting. With the spiritual backing of Gerebern she again refuses to obey her father. Upon which the king, incensed, decapitates his daughter with his sword, and the soldiers slay the priest

Ciborium in the St-Dimpnakerk

Statue of St Dymphna, Augustinian abbey, Tongerlo.

Old hospital in Geel, now the Gasthuismuseum.

likewise. The Irish king departs, natives come and, deploring the fugitives' fate, bury them in empty Roman sarcophagi of the chapel of Saint Martin. As to the innkeeper's wife in Westerlo, she is left paralysed, an extended arm pointing in the direction of the hermitage . . . !

In the twenty-one panels of the altar-piece in Saint Dymphna's church in Geel visitors will find this legend skilfully portrayed (plate 5). Dymphna is also especially revered in the Augustinian abbey of Tongerlo, two kilometres from Westerlo. Geel itself — could the name come from *gealt*, the Irish for 'mad'? — has been titled 'The Town of Compassion' because of its untiring social commitments. In the late 19th century some three thousand patients were counted in the parishioners' personal care.

Royalty expresses its devotion inside the 14th-century church with a copper plaque confirming the attendance of King Albert of Belgium at the Saint Dymphna celebrations of the year 1900. There, numerous statues, paintings and stained glass windows represent the patron saint and also Saint Gerebern, who has a side-altar to himself. The main attraction is however the ciborium — the object of a ritual, resembling that of the Eastern Church, which a person seeking a cure has to observe nine times. This consists of creeping through the narrow passage under the ciborium. On the pillared stone receptacle shielding the 13th-century oak coffin box with the relics of both saints, scenes of the martyrdom are painted in renaissance style. In the coffin are also preserved the remnants of the sarcophagi that originally entombed the saints.

A further unique feature in Saint Dymphna's church in Geel is its ancient sickroom, the *Sieckencamere*. In it the mentally disabled are expected to spend nine days in prayer and meditation — locked in, if necessary! The chamber in its present form dates from the year 1683.

With the dispersal of the canons in the French Revolution, the attachment of the people of Geel to their 'Dimpnakerk' was sorely put to the test. Confiscated, it was put up for sale, but through subscriptions they were able to buy it back.

Dymphna, upheld as a martyr in the name of chastity and fortitude, is portrayed mostly with her foot on a chained demon. This in accordance with the ancient belief, that madness is caused by attacks of the devil, intent on driving human beings out of their senses, so as to take possession of their souls. That Satan can be extirpated by the intercession of Dymphna is the mystery of Geel.

Was it once so in Ireland's *Tech Damnata*? For those further interested in the subject, there is the Geeler museum in the Gasthuisstraat. It is here that, as the name of the street indicates, the 15th century infirmary stood, superseding the original 13th-century hospital. The building now houses the museum.

SAARLAND AND THE
PALATINATE

It was the intention of Clovis' son Theuderich, who came to the throne in 511, to strengthen – or widen – the boundaries of Austrasia, the part of the Empire he had inherited, by regenerating the spiritual life of Trier with a reinforcement of clerics from Aquitaine. In this scheme Fridolin may have been included. Trier became the focus of missionary activity and served as a training centre. A Roman road would take a missionary from Aquitaine past Bourges to Rheims and on to Trier – where, however, Fridolin did not remain. Fired by his mission, his aim was the conversion of the Alemanni in the East. Facilities were available for downstream traffic on the Rhine tributaries, Saar and Mosel, and Fridolin halted on the left bank of the winding Mosel, where today a small wine resort bears the corrupted form of the *cella* he founded – Eller (Saint Hilaire = Helera). Then, driven by the visionary promise of an island sanctuary among the heathens, Fridolin moves on, perhaps towards the Rhine confluence, where an ancient highway leading south awaited him. On this upstream path many Irish feet were to follow.

No one interested in Early Christian Europe can afford to overlook Trier (Trèves) where in the year 325 Constantine the Great built his cathedral. There Fridolin's name appears in a litany of the 10th century, the period of the Lorraine Reform, a movement in which Irish abbots played their part in the great schools of Trier and Metz. Long before that, Irish-styled monasticism had entered and influenced Trier, this ancient Roman capital with its colonies of foreigners, inherited by the Merovingians. Saint Maximin's abbey, that stood outside the city walls, had strong Columban associations, storing the oldest available manuscript of the *Navigatio Sancti Brendani*, and providing an abbot's list

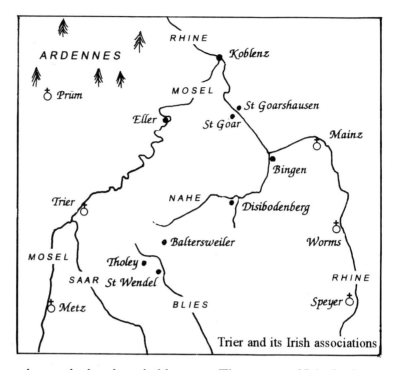

Trier and its Irish associations

that goes back to the early 6th century. The nunnery of Saint Irminen-Oeren, installed in the shell of a Roman warehouse on the Mosel embankment before 639, was affiliated to Remirement, the Columban double monastery on the upper Mosel (Vosges). The equally old Trier convent Saint Symphorian also had connexions with Burgundy, while from Aquitaine hailed the great 6th-century reformer bishop Nicetius, who greatly favoured Saint Maximin's. A former abbot, Nicetius no doubt promoted establishments of *cellae* and rural *monasteria* of Irish design in his vast diocese.

If the Christian Faith did not fail in the region after the Roman retreat in 475, its continuity must be attributed to the stamina of the bishops who stayed on, holding their own in episcopal bastions such as Mainz and Worms on the Rhine, and Trier – pillars of civilization from which the church could operate. And it was from these authorities, now primarily concerned with the restoration of the dioceses, that a *peregrinus* had to obtain permission for erecting some modest quarters of his own and ministering to the common people. The *peregrini* were the

Trier, seen from the vineyards across the Mosel river (Cornelius Visscher, 1650).

Eller, on the Mosel.

81

Collegiate church, St Goer.
On the opposite bank,
St Goarshausen.

foot-soldiers of the Christian campaign, pushing in across the Ardennes range and the Palatinate towards the Rhine, with the Alemanni and other barbaric tribes beyond. Tradition has preserved for us knowledge of a few such pioneers – Beatus, Disibod, Wendelin and Goar having survived as place-names – cherished in folk memory as Irish hermits missioning in the region.

And so we find Saint Goar (Guaire?) arriving from Aquitaine in 519 to establish himself in the wilds east of Trier, where he applies for permission for a station, or hermitage, on the left bank of the Rhine. The site he chose – where the present town of Sankt Goar stands – was not incidental but full of purpose. For this was at a point on the river where since prehistoric times people had crossed over; including the Romans, in whose forsaken post Goar could settle. And there he built a hostel. The Rhine, having forced a cleavage between precipitous cliffs, is here at its narrowest, making a curve between rocks, partly submerged, that later gave rise to Lorelei fantasies. This was a danger zone, where help was welcome, and Goar knew that he would encounter here the simple people he wished to convert – fishermen, boatsmen, travellers from both sides of the current. That he himself practised the ferryman's task is not pure legend, for the little town on the opposite bank answers to the name 'Sankt Goarshausen'.

Tradition also affirms that Goar practised the use of his bell to steer navigators off the rocks when taking the dreaded corner. Up to the 19th century it was customary for Rhine boatsmen to ring a bell and say a prayer to Saint Goar when passing the strait with the Lorelei rock above. This custom only died with the blasting of the reefs in 1825, making the passage available for steamers.

Out of Goar's hermitage – the *cella sancti Goaris* frequented by Carolingian kings and commoners – a toll station developed, bringing prosperity to the narrow strip along the shore, above which towers the castle that guarded it: Rheinfels, now housing an interesting museum. But in Goar's day, fishermen, thirsty bargemen and weary wanderers were glad to find a welcome in the hermit's hostel, where three hinds were kept to provide milk for guests. The concourse became so great that suspicion arose in Trier that wine and not milk was the cause of this popularity. Two spies were dispatched by the bishop to investigate. Having found nothing to support the rumour, the men lost their way on the return journey through the dense forest and would have expired but for an inexplicable provision of fresh milk discovered in their baggage!

However, alarmed by further reports of miracles, and jealous perhaps of Goar's success, the authorities summoned the hermit to appear before the bishop's court in Trier. There Goar accounted for himself by performing the feat of Saint Brigid and Saint Brendan. He hung his cloak up in the hall on a sunbeam, thus convincing the synod of the sanctity of his calling.

Of the many delightful legends of this beloved apostle, iconography presents a few. Goar is portrayed with his cloak, often with his three hinds and a jar of milk. He carries either a model of the church he founded, or a key, signifying the hospitality offered (plate 6). A demon is sometimes posed on his shoulder, or under his foot – a reminder of the sorcery, of which he was unjustly accused.

The later *Monasterium St. Goaris Confessoris* on the Rhine was the summer residence of the abbots of Prüm, itself affiliated to Saint Faro's abbey in Meaux. The present collegiate church was built in the early 15th century on the site of Goar's original chapel, where he died in 575, or 611. The great cult that brought pilgrims to the saint's tomb, came to a sudden end with the Reformation, and the large sepulchral crypt under the church is empty. But people long continued to visit the *cella* by the little stream that here flows into the Rhine, where a cave can be seen, cut out of the rock – the nucleus of it all.

Saint Goar belongs to the category of saints whose reputation relies

St Goar performing the sunbeam miracle (17th-century engraving).

83

St Wendalin's cenotaph in the choir of St Wendel's basilica (c. 1400).

mainly on oral tradition, proving him to be a true saint of the people. Such sources are certainly no less reliable than late biographies. Apart from these tales, songs, ballads and shanties have stored the image of a missionary whose traits seem unmistakably those of the Irish *peregrinus* folk memory recalls – even if he shares his name with a tribal king of the Alanen! Goar is the patron saint of ferrymen, Rhine boatsmen, and of innkeepers.

With the exception of the 11th-century saint Koloman, no saint of Irish reputation ever appealed to the imagination of peoples of German stock, or met with such public devotion in country communities, as did Saint Wendalin (Vindelinus, Waldolen, etc.). Suebian colonists took his cult eastward into regions of the Lower Danube, and in emigrant ships to North America it was brought into the New World. From the Netherlands to South Tyrol, wherever a Germanic tongue could be heard, but especially in lands of Alemannic heritage, sanctuaries dedicated to 'Sankt Wendalin' were strewn. Fifteen hundred churches under his patronage have been counted, beside at least five hundred and fifty chapels. Pilgrimages took place regularly to around one hundred and sixty of these sites, but most are now extinct.

84

The beginning of the cult can be located in the hilly country to the south of Trier in one-time Austrasia, where the rivers Nahe and Blies rise. There Wendalin's tomb graces the beautiful late-Gothic basilica of Saint Wendalin, that gave his name both to the town of Sankt Wendel and to the surrounding country: 'Sankt Wendalin's Land'.

A true saint of the people, Wendalin's oral tradition is strong. This is backed by documentation that, while verifying his existence as a contemporary of bishop Magnerich of Trier who died in 596, does not hesitate to compare him with such Irish patriarchs as Columban and Gall. Wendalin's own demise is generally given as the year 617. To what Irish father 'king of the Scoti' refers is not known – perhaps his son's name was Fintan (Vindalin)?

What folk memory has stored for us is the image of a prince who, forfeiting his rights, chose to live among the lowest and humblest, as a hermit of the woods. In Tholey, twelve kilometres from Sankt Wendel, he spent his last years as head of a monastic community, it is said. The saint's grave is in Sankt Wendel, but the Benedictine abbey of Tholey, a foundation of the year 1000, where the monks still use Gregorian chant, is well restored and worth a visit. Above the abbey a volcanic hilltop now called the Schaumberg was in turn a Celtic *oppidum*, a Roman *castrum* and a Merovingian fortress. It was then in the early 7th century that Adalgisel-Grimo, a deacon of the Franks, caused a church to be built in memory of Wendalin in the valley below. Traces of a rectangular building, probably Adalgisel's *Eigenkirche* (church owned by the nobility) were discovered underneath the choir of the present abbey church of Tholey, the entire complex of which stands on the site of a Roman bath. Indeed, the stones of the thermal structure may first have prompted Wendalin to build his cell here.

Wendalin's cult reached a new height in the late Middle Ages, when plagues swept the land, sparing only Sankt Wendel, that had enjoyed his patronage since 1050. A larger pilgrim's church was the result, and the installation of the saint's relics there in 1360 became a feastday held ever after and celebrated in the whole archdiocese of Trier.

Pilgrims still pass behind the high altar of Saint Wendel's basilica, underneath the raised sarcophagus of beautifully ornamented sandstone containing the saint's reliquary (plate 23). In the choir stands the so-called *tumba*, a cenotaph serving as a table for the exposure of the

St Wendalin in 18th-century rococo attire. St Kilian's church, Pretzfeld, Franconia.

85

*Benedictine abbey of Tholey, at
the foot of the Schaumberg hill.*

reliquary on occasions. It, too, has notable carvings of Gothic design, including the oldest image of Wendalin known to exist – a youthful *peregrinus* clasping his *cambutta*; beside him in the adjoining panel the admiring donor offers a huge candle (plate 7). Very impressive is a 20th-century addition that forms the lid of the *tumba*, a bronze image of the saint lying in death. Three sheep are grouped mourning at the faithful guardian's head – Wendalin, protector of flocks, herds and their pastures.

This leads us to the core of the legend. Wendalin, disgraced in the eyes of his father for refusing to take on princely duties, is degraded to the cast of a simple herdsman. Upon which he takes his departure, leaving Ireland with six friends on a pilgrimage of no return. Having decided to follow in Christ's footsteps by renouncing the world and its riches, Wendalin is next heard of when reaching the lands of the Middle Rhine, after visiting Rome. Somewhere near the Roman road from Bingen to Trier he builds himself a hut of green branches, then he sets out to visit the martyrs' graves in the famous *Sancta Treviris*. On the road he is noticed by a passing horseman, the pagan lord of Tholey, who mistaking Wendalin for a beggar, scoffs at his idle behaviour, remarking that herdsmen were much in demand, but not lazy-bones asking for alms. Taking these words as a sign of God, Wendalin takes up service with the pagan lord; first as his swineherd, then his cowherd, at length his shepherd.

Once, when crossing the distant wilds of his domain, the horseman encounters Wendalin with his sheep among the trees, and he angrily reprimands him for leading the flock so far astray – 'I have visitors tonight,' says he, 'and what shall I now serve them with, since a lamb for the feast is not available? You cannot reach the farm before nightfall!'

To his great surprise, on returning home the master finds Wendalin there before him, leading the sheep through the courtyard gate. Struck by this supernatural occurrence, he begs his shepherd for forgiveness, convinced that he is indeed a saintly person. Refusing to let Wendalin continue living in servitude, he offers riches and a contrite heart, but Wendalin will accept only his Christian vows and, taking the wages that are his due, returns to his forest cell, where he distributes them to the poor.

The legendary cave is still shown, near Baltersweiler to the north-east of Tholey, where Wendalin with his flock took their mysterious short cut back to the farm of the pagan lord!

86

The 14th-century Wendalinus-Basilica is one of Germany's most perfect period churches, the pride of the Saarland. In the market-place beyond stands a graceful 18th-century fountain with a statue of the church's patron. The town of Saint Wendel is the centre of the cult, and celebrations on the shepherd-saint's feastday in October include a fair held there that lasts a week, called the Wendalinus Markt. From here a fifteen minutes' walk takes us to Saint Wendalin's well (plate 21). The chapel beside it is seldom without a lighted candle within. And what, in truth, is an Irish saint's legend worth without a miraculous spring of water? It is affirmed that a great drought hit the region during Wendalin's lifetime, and when people turned to him for help, he struck the ground on this spot with his *cambutta*. The spring that gushed forth has flowed ever since down a valley called after him. There each year up to 500 horses and tractors(!) are brought to be blessed (plate 15), while pilgrims sing the incantations of their forefathers in praise of 'Wendalin mild', the 'gentle, the indulgent', also called a 'chapel saint' because of the profusion of santuaries erected in his name for the protection of the land, scattered around in meadows, on slopes, in silvan settings. Anywhere secluded grazing for farm animals is available we meet these tiny oratories, adorned invariably with an image of a youth kneeling with his staff, his crown in the grass beside him — the fairy-tale saint that loved the lowest and humblest of the human race, proud to consider him their very own. And they chant:

O hoher, edler Königssohn, Sankt Wendalin!
Verließest Heimat Du und Thron, Sankt Wendalin!
Siechtum und Plagen
Von uns wolltest jagen,
Sankt Wendalin!
(O noble, gracious monarch's son, Saint Wendalin!/For us forsook-est home and throne, Saint Wendalin!/from us to disperse/disease and distress/ Saint Wendalin!)

Among the missionaries, martyrs and dignitaries of ancient Trier there are two, professed to be of Irish origin, who have left their names on heights in the region — Beatus and Disibodus. Of the former we know little more than that he had his hermitage on the hill of Beatenberg near

87

St Wendalin's Valley,
Saarland.

Koblenz on the Rhine, where through his deeds and devotions many were converted to the Christian Faith.

Disibodus is better off. Not only did he leave his name on Disibodenberg, near Bingen, a little further up the Rhine from Sankt Goar but there exists a 12th-century *Vita Sancti Disibodi*, written by the celebrated 'Sibyl of the Rhine', Saint Hildegard of Bingen, who spent half her life in the nunnery of the great Benedictine abbey evolving out of Disibod's hermitage that topped the hill. Also at our disposal is a chronicle assembled by 12th-century monks of Disibodenberg Abbey, the *Annales Sancti Disibodi*.

Hildegard's Life of Saint Disibod, more a Book of Revelation than a biography, provides us with secondhand information of a fantastic nature. But if the Irish background in it lacks authenticity, other traditions passed down in the monastery may have been available to Hildegard and inspired her in her medicinal studies, the fruits of which are still greatly valued. The stress laid on a herbarium for the culture of curative plants is especially noticeable in medieval monasteries with Irish traditions.

What greets our Irish visitor to Disibodenberg today is a wooded hill (out of the crest of which two gables protrude) that juts out in the angle formed by the confluence of the Glan and Nahe rivers. The solitary mound is a landmark in the valley. A road on its south side, flanked with vineyards, brings us up the incline, and halfway up lies a farmhouse, the Disibodenberger Hof, with its museum. Traditionally the spot where Disibod built his first cell and oratory, it is also the place where he was, at his own wish for a 'humble burial', first interred. The monastery, already expanding during Disbod's lifetime, had been moved up to the hilltop plateau, and to its church the saint's remains were brought when, out of this nucleus, a centre developed on which the religious life of the entire region was for centuries to focus. Destroyed, abandoned and forgotten, its ruins were re-discovered by 19th-century tourists, and romantic sketches made by artists were etched and engraved. Since then, the spacious monastic area has had an assessment made of its buildings, and the survey of the years 1985–90 has paved the way for archeological research to include the whole plateau, as yet only superficially probed.

Saint Disibod was treated with great veneration of old, especially in

the diocese of Trier. Folklore, however, never adopted him with the fervour shown towards Goar and Wendelin, two local missionaries also reputed to have hailed from Ireland. But tradition records Disibod's clemency and his healing powers and the ministry of his disciples to the poor.

Already a bishop when leaving Ireland with a small attendance, Disibod was an elderly man on appearing in the Rhine province of 7th-century Gaul. His whereabouts before this and the route he took are not known. In Trier he was offered a site by Merovingian rulers.

As tradition insists on the missionary character of Disibod's *monasterium*, it may be that the Irishman was a tool of Franconian church policy, which had as its aim the consolidation of a chain of bishoprics along the Rhine, taken over from the Romans; thus strengthening the empire borderlands in the North-east, where barbarian aggression permanently loomed. Primarily serving a strategy of defence, the archiepiscopal seat of Mainz and with it the see of Trier were now spearheads in the campaign of evangelizing tribes across the Rhine in *Teutonica Francia*. And since Disibodenberg with its surrounding territory was

Disibodenberg. The hilltop monastic ruins.

Sandstone image of Disibod (?) found in the cloister ruins, 1990.

89

12th-century cover design of St Hilde-gard's Vita sancti Disibodi, *reproduced in the Acta Sanctorum of the Bollandists, 1887. Illustrating the Disibod legend, it includes the saint's three Irish companions (top), his apostolate, his healing powers and the concourse of pilgrims at his ornate tomb.*

part of a donation to the archbishop of Mainz by Merovingian royalty, Disibod's church was a royal abbey (*Eigenkirche*) and subject to this policy. We may conclude that our Irishman was invited to Trier, along with those dignitaries brought in from Poitou and the Merovingian enclave in Aquitaine, on a moral reinforcement project for the Rhineland.

Another suggestion put forward is that Disibod belonged to the party of Saint Kilian, who crossed the Rhine and died in Würzburg in 689. Whatever the case, legend has it had Disibod's journey from Ireland to Gaul was directed by an angel who revealed that he would found a monastery 'where two rivers meet'. To the east of Trier, in the valley south of the Hunsrück range Disibod found the angular flat-topped mountain of his vision where the Glan meets the Nahe, soon to join the Rhine at Bingen, and here he lived and laboured with his little troop, dying at the then biblical age of 81. His grave was soon a resort for pilgrims, with his church crowning the hill.

That Disibodenberg suffered under Viking and Hungarian incursions of the 9th and 10th centuries is known from the reported visit of the archbishop of Mainz to the mountain sanctuary in 975. Dismayed at the 'desolate state of the buildings and grave of Disibodus', he caused twelve canons to be installed there. The Augustinian Friars, ever keen admirers of the Irish mission that matched their own precepts of charitable and spiritual engagement, did much to cement the cult of Disibod in the region, and they fastened his image in the minds of the people as an apostolic Irish founder-saint.

This was to remain when, a hundred years later, Benedictines took over what was now a double monastery, to be followed in 1259 by Cistericans from the Palatinate who remained until 1559. It was the abbey's richest period. A magnificent basilica now crowned the hill, the centre of the founder's cult, whose remains together with those of his three companions were displayed in an ornate marble sarcophagus at the high altar.

Endless wars and turmoils beset the walled-in monastery, mostly caused by land claims of the gentry, contested by the episcopate. Again the Benedictines tried their luck. They managed to hold their own in the stronghold throughout the Thirty Years' War, but were subsequently forced to flee. The Abbey, left to decay, was officially declared a stone quarry in the 18th century and dismantled. While fragments from its library are scattered everywhere, specimens of its stone masonry can be seen in the surrounding villages, some items showing Roman design. — It had happened as in Burgundy, where Columban's monks made use of the Roman stones of their predecessors on the sacred hill of Annegray.

THE MAINSTREAM
(OBERRHEIN) AND ALSACE

Surrounding oneself with water is a typically Irish defence strategy. An islet in a lake, or flowing stream, artificial or not, real or on stilts, afforded refuge to the Island Celt in his troubled history, although not interminably. After the warriors and their families, came the monks with their chants, seeking peace for meditation, or leisure to develop into a missionary centre — Dair Inis, for example, in the mouth of the Blackwater, its monastery associated with Lismore, both in close contact with the Continent until their final destruction.

This strategy was copied by the Irish abroad. On the river Rhine alone, five island settlements of the *scotti peregrini* were noted.

In Cologne there is no trace left of the original church of Saint Martin, since the place on which it stood in Merovingian times ceased to be an island. But we are aware of its erection, probably a wooden sanctuary replacing a Roman chapel, this in its turn replacing a pagan temple. To make way for a fortified market area near the port, the side-arm of the Rhine beyond which Saint Martin stood was filled in during the 10th century, and a larger church was erected over old Roman warehouses to replace it. Soon given over to Irish Benedictines, the new Saint Martin's had an adjoining chapel dedicated to Saint Brigid, which became the parish church of 'Sankt Brigiden', as well as an Irish abbey on the market place beyond.

This development could imply that the former Saint Martin's was also entrusted to the Irish. Of this there is scant reference, which cannot be verified. As in the case of the Irish island monastery of Honau, it went down in the waves, and with it the history of its origin.

In Cologne, however, 'Great Saint Martin', as it is called, has

Cologne in 1531, a woodcut by A. Woensams. In the centre, Great St Martin dominates the scene. To its left, the low spire of the parish church of St Brigid.

survived. Scarred, burned, besieged, destroyed and lovingly rebuilt again, it stands, as the city's imposing landmark on the river front. It also stands as a fascinating reminder of the early Irish presence there, in the very heart of 'Sancta, sacrosancta Colonia', after Merovingian kings took up residence on the cathedral hill.

Columban's itinerary does not include Cologne. His destination, after the injuries suffered in Gaul, was Rome, but in Metz Theudebert II urged him to stay in Austrasia, offering him the apostolate of a barbaric region in the far East of his kingdom. Only recently occupied by the Suebian tribe of the Alemanni, this was a country Columban would have to traverse, in order to pass over the Alps into Italy.

Columban's journey thither, leading him up the Rhine, is famed by the *'carmen navale'*, a boat-song in eight verses attributed to him – a sophisticated Latin composition, urging the oarsmen on, as they row up the river. However sturdy the crew, and much as we wish to admire those Irish and Breton monks, it is hard to envisage them battling successfully with the crags and whirlpools beneath the Lorelei, on an upstream passage! The boat in question, provided by the Austrasian king in 610, was more likely supplied for taking them down the river Mosel. At Koblenz a well-trodden Roman road awaited them, leading them down south to the Alps.

Bicornis Hreni, mentioned in the second verse of the boat-song, is generally translated 'the two-horned Rhine', which conveys nothing. But the other Latin meaning for *bicornis*, 'the twofold estuary', describes perfectly the twin arms of the Waal and the Lek rivers, into which the Rhine branches just below Nimwegen. This was the Roman 'Noviomagus', a settlement whose occupants were surely aware of the nature of the district, with the juncture beyond, into which Julius Caesar preferred not to penetrate. Yonder was the homeland of the Frisians, a barbarous people never taken into account by Columban. But perhaps Frisian boatsmen had a ditty, taken over and improved on by the legionaries of the Lower Rhine? Jonas, Columban's biographer, may have been bold enough to use this, transferring its authorship to his hero.

Columban's itinerary, passing from Gaul to Italy, as given by Jonas is meagre enough. His stop in Mainz is noted, but nothing further down the road that trailed up the left bank of the Rhine to Basel. The diversion then taken is known to us from the biographers of Columban's companion Saint Gall.

Mainz, where the party obtained provisions from a bishop Leonisus, had by 610 recovered from its post-Roman disturbances and become a thriving Merovingian commercial and missionary centre. Here an 8th-century Irish abbot of the Rhine island of Honau built his church and drew up a deed confirming his *paruchia* – eight foundations of Hesse to the North, all with Irish dignitaries at their head. Ireland maintained long and outstanding connexions with this ancient metropolis, a relationship of scholarly interest, but primarily apostolic. The sites of its various institutes are, however, irrevocably lost. After World War II, in which Mainz suffered an 80 per cent. destruction, the city core has been painstakingly rebuilt, but two Irish abbeys still operating in the middle of the 18th century are gone with the rest. All we will find there are a few street-names, such as *Schottstrasse* and *Altmünstergasse* marking the route of the Roman highway that led west out of the city. Just beyond bounds, beside the Roman city wall, there stood around the year 700 the Irish monastery Saint Paul, and a nunnery with a dedication to Saint Brigid. Their place on the periphery confirms the principles of the *hospitalia Scoti* to cater for the wayfarer, the pilgrim, the outcast, and to minister to the country folk. Significantly, these charitable traditions were, in Mainz as elsewhere, taken over later by 'Brigiden convents' of the Beginen Society, one of which still operates in the vicinity.

The 'Bishop's church' in Mainz that Columban entered was presumably Sankt Johannis. Standing to the west of the cathedral, it is considered to be the oldest bishop's seat in town. Badly mutilated, what remains of the chancel is restored and modernized. The Irish visitor is advised to take cheer and resort to the city museums, where our period is exceptionally well represented.

Old town maps show a 'St. Gallus' chapel seated on the embankment straight under the cathedral. It was there in the year 1300, but its history is unknown.

A group of Irish monks following the Rule of Columban were granted the island of Honau – Hohe Aue, the upper isle, Latinized *Honaugia* – in the year 722. The donor, in accordance with his Franconian overlords was Alabert, Alemannic ruler of the dynasty of Eticho.

Tradition affirms that it was the Irish Saint Er(h)ard, through his connections with the Alsatian Etichon dynasty, who brought about this donation, and that Erhard himself presented relics of Saint Brigid to the Columban island community on its foundation. He also deposited relics of the saint in Strassburg (Strasbourg), thirteen kilometres away, where the 14th-century church of Saint-Érard still remembers him. Standing near the site of the old Roman port on the river Ill, the Rhine tributary that embraces the original city centre, it serves an old hospital.

The activities of Honau's missionaries earned their abbey such respect that a series of charters were issued by Alemannic and Franconian rulers, including Charlemagne, confirming its property, its rights and privileges, which included exemption from toll. Apart from their island patron, Saint Michael, the monks showed special veneration for Saint Brigid. She was given a chapel of her own, and the custom was upheld of distributing free meals to the poor on her feastday.

Churches built in her honour in the incumbency of Saint Michael have left the region a remarkable number of parishes under her patronage, her cult radiating from Honau into Baden, along the border of the Black Forest on the right side of the Rhine, as well as into Alsace. Carried northward to Mainz and beyond, we find, among other places, a town in Hesse(n) echoing its 8th-century Irish colony from Honau with the name 'Schotten'. Dedicated to Saint Michael, the original wooden church with its altar to Saint Brigid has long since gone, but in the Reformed Church building that superseded it, two 'scotic' virgins hold her place in a modern window-painting behind the high altar.

In the year 1290 enterprise came to an end. Due to inundation, the monks of Honau – now Augustinian friars – were forced to quit their Rhine sanctuary. They were compensated with an island further up the river, which they also dedicated to Saint Michael (Rheinau).

Opposite Honau, in the Ortenau on the right bank of the Rhine under the Black Forest range, the old church tower of Sankt Brigitta in Sasbach signals the Irish fugitives' first stop on that sad day, leaving, it

96

is believed, a relic of their patroness here. But when in the 18th century the parish of Sasbach got its new church – a very beautiful one – it ignored its origins, re-dedicating Sankt Brigitta to the then popular Birgit of Sweden – a 14th-century nun who died in Rome!

Columban, following the upstream course of the Rhine from Mainz, could not as yet appreciate these Christian cells he was to inspire, or see the early Carolingian Lorsch, standing on the far side of the river. Of this influential royal abbey only the impressive 'Torhalle' remains; but in the annals salvaged from its great library a list of 8th-century Irish abbots has come down to us, as well as a Hiberno-Latin grammar and some Irish manuscript remains of the 9th century. A 10th-century massbook of Lorsch contains a proper for Saint Brigid, who enjoyed for ages, among other localities, the patronage of the nearby Bürstadt. Further south in the Ortenau stood the great Benedictine abbey of Schwarzach. Its remaining church, a 13th-century architectural jewel, stands on the site of what was probably the *ecclesia Scottorum* transplanted from the Rhine island of Arnulfsau in the Rhine swamps. We have knowledge of that original island site from a document of the year 748 confirming its rights, issued by Etto, the bishop of Strasbourg whom we will meet again in connection with Landelin. Dubán, the then Irish abbot-bishop of Honau, was one of the signatories of the deed.

On the road from Schwarzach to Strasbourg we pass Rheinau-Freistett with its early Romanesque 'Church of the Heathens' – a reminder of the busy monks of Honau on their island beyond. Then comes a place today named Honau, with its 19th-century church dedicated faithfully to Saint Michael who also had the patronage of the first parish church of Schwarzach, Sankt Michaelis. In the adjacent Stollhofen another Irish association is upheld in the parish church of Sankt Erhard – a consistency to compensate us for the Sasbach *lapsus*!

The church of St Erhard, Stollhofen.

Did Columban visit Strasbourg when passing? A very old Strasbourg tradition affirms that he did, and that he even ministered in Alsace, linking his name to the church of Saint Peter, called 'the Young' to distinguish it from another ancient church in the city known as 'Old Saint Peter'. Both stood originally outside the walls of *Strata-burgum*, or *Stradeburgo*, the 'road fortress' of an old Roman route that went on

13th-century fresco of St Columban (restored). Church of Young St Peter, Strasbourg.

to form a junction with another at the Rhine crossing beyond. This strategically important citadel changed hands from the Celts to the Romans into those of the Alemanni, to become Strassburg (= Strasbourg). It stood on an island formed by the Ill, still enclosing the city's core in an almond-shaped frame, a limitation of great advantage to the visitor of early ecclesiastical sites, for the extent never exceeds two kilometres. Our objects of interest are all within walking distance of each other — a stroll around the wharfs, enhanced by many bridges.

It was here that Julius Caesar vanquished the Suevi, a Germanic tribal confederation in 58 BC. But after the fall of the Roman Empire, they won the bridgehead back again, crossing the Rhine this time for good. Pouring into Alsace they settled mainly in the south of that fruitful country, sharing it henceforth with the Franks to the north — Clovis and his sons wisely allowing them to keep their own ethnic rulers.

Strasbourg had been a 4th-century Roman episcopal see, and, with a new society now emerging, it had to cope with the work of restoration — a great call for moral and spiritual incentive, such as the monasticism of Luxeuil had to offer. Luxeuil was to form the mainstay of Merovingian church policy, especially during the reigns of Chlotar II and Dagobert I, a period from 584–639, and out of this function the Alemanni mission developed. From Burgundy and across the Vosges mountains Columban's disciples trudged — no problem for Luxeuil which, by the middle of the 7th century, was overflowing with inmates. Fanning out in all directions they were founding churches and missionary stations, nowhere more intensely than in Alsace.

It is therefore not surprising to find reports of a wooden church of that period set up by Irish monks outside the city gates of Strasbourg, for the benefit of the natives. It included an asylum for the poor and for passing pilgrims. Apart from its typically Irish motivation, this *extra muros* position casts a sorry light on the inherent Roman attitude to religion, practised exclusively within colonial walls, where even a different jurisdiction held sway.

This scant bit of information from indigenous sources concerning a modest *monasterium scottorum* found unexpected backing with a discovery made during the restoration of the church of Saint Peter the Young at the turn of the 19th century. The installation of heating pipes

98

revealed an underground vault full of human bones in tombs of the early Christian period. (The sarcophagi can be viewed in the grounds of a municipal building nearby.) The burial chamber lay just beyond the precincts of a former church built in 1031, and had obviously been filled in when the much larger present church was erected in Gothic style in the period 1250–1320. The site is open to the public.

Reformed, Young Saint Peter was given a 19th-century neo-Gothic coating that has all but obliterated the complex character of its history. The base of the tower, and part of the cloisters are Romanesque, and a 13th-century fresco of Saint Columban, albeit restored, recalls the Augustinian traditional devotion to Irish origins – old archives of Saint Peter confirming that here stood, indeed, a church dedicated to the saint of Luxeuil.

Our difficulty is discerning whether Columban's connection with Young Saint Peter was personal or not. The burial vault, over which supposedly the wooden Irish church stood, may have been in use before his transit, when Merovingian kings first took recourse to the services of missionaries in their programme of integrating Alemannic settlers on the left bank of the Rhine in their empire, and of strengthening the episcopate in Strasbourg. Before following other traces in this respect, let us first see where those Honau refugees eventually landed, together with the shrines of their holy abbots and other relics – in the church of Strasbourg's 'Old Saint Peter'.

A short walk along the quay brings us to the one-time collegiate church that offered an end to that Odyssey in the year 1348, after the second island of the Honau monks was undermined by currents of the Rhine. This Augustinian house in Strasbourg, only recently re-erected, they also named Saint Michael's. To the left of the doorway a stone effigy of Saint Brigid looks down on the traffic – herself having suffered mutilation when a bomb of the Second World War blew off her hand. With the monks, her cult came to this church, together with some treasured relic. We cannot, however, accept that this was her *head*, or that the skull revered in the Catholic part of the church (now serving two denominations) belongs to Brigid! If we allow for the possibility of Saint Gall and Saint Erhard bringing relics from Kildare to these parts in early times, it would be preposterous to suppose that anything as important as her head would have been taken from its sepulchre before Viking depredations of the 9th century made the removal of the saint's remains necessary – by which time the Irish monks were well established on the island of Honau!

During the French Revolution the treasures of Old Saint Peter were robbed, the contents of the gold and silver reliquaries scattered. Hidden and later restored to the altars, what remains of these relics was exposed again to veneration by the bishop of Strasbourg in 1806. Among them in its new reliquary, the 'head of Saint Brigid' should be treated with reserve.

This does not however rule out the possibility of the skull belonging to an Irish namesake, that of a companion of Saint Ursula, martyred in Cologne. Relics of the virgin saints in company of Saint Ursula were in great demand in the Middle Ages, several of which are listed in the inventory of Honau.

For those curious to view the spot where this island abbey stood before succumbing to the floods, a road to the north of Strasbourg leads to the village of Wantzenau on the Ill, that flows into the Rhine near *Kilstett*, the 'Place of the Cill'. Here a bridge crosses over to *Freistett*, the 'Place of Asylum', joining Alsace with the province of Baden-Württemberg in Germany. Hither and thither, place-names reveal traces of Honau's pastoral activities in the vicinity.

Strasbourg being not seated directly on the Rhine, river barges trading with the city used the waterways of the Ill tributary to reach it. On passing Wantzenau a Roman boat of the 3rd century capsized, coming to light again in the 20th century with vestiges of its cargo and some coins. The Ill landing-place in Strasbourg is thought to have been near where the great monastic school of Saint Thomas flourished in medieval times.

Attached to the present-day protestant church of Sankt Thomas, this institute accommodates a seminary of theology, a spiritual heritage of Franco-Irish missionary zeal. For it was here that Saint Florentius, bishop of Strasbourg in the late 6th century, founded the abbey, called by chroniclers 'the cradle of Christianity in Alsace'. Florentius, given Irish origin of noble birth by his biographers, claims to be the first to bring the Faith to these parts. He chose this place, then just outside the city walls, for his missionary station, for the convenience of country folk, flocking to the tomb of his predecessor bishop Arbogast, also reputed to be Irish. Tradition recalls this site as one of early Christian baptisms, a *monasterium scottorum* related also in some way with Saint Columban and having an altar to Saint Brigid. Rebuilt by bishop Adeloch in the 9th century, it was re-dedicated to Saint Thomas, and so it has remained. A whole series of devastations, caused mainly by fire, has left at least the Carolingian sepulchre of Adeloch intact in the church choir.

Sankt Thomas, with its stern 12th-century tower, next to the cathedral the most salient of Strasbourg's religious edifices, heads the city's protestant community. Its interior reveals architectural features of many periods. At the Romanesque doorway into the chapel of Saint Blasius we encounter a fresco on the wall portraying Saint Florentius restoring a lamb, stolen by a wolf, to its owner. This popular legend has since been attached to the later cult of Saint Blasius, also a tamer of animals. Equally called into question is the Irish provenance of Saint Arbogast, and even that of Florentius is sometimes doubted, in spite of his references. The main stumbling-block in these cases being their non-Irish names, it might be pointed out that it was the aim of Irish missionaries to adapt themselves soundly to their environment, and this applied also to their names, so often changed or contorted. Florentius may well have been christened Blathmac, a name met often in Irish monastery files, that he used in a Latin translation.

The scarcity of 6th-century documentary evidence does indeed cloud the path of those pioneer days when Arbogast and Florentius laboured in Alsace, starting we are told with hermitages, to be consequently called to the see of Strasbourg by Merovingian kings. Let us wander out into the country and see what else folk memory has to offer to support our early apostles. Alsace is rich in edifices and images that strengthen their claim.

Arbogast and Florentius are treated with awe in the 10th-century 'Life of Saint Dicuil', a chronicle from the Columban abbey of Lure. They are noted as supreme religious leaders, 'the holiest of all Strasbourg's holy patrons'. Arbogast's arrival in Alsace is accepted as being in the year 550, his bishopric being proceeded by a sojourn in the forest of Hagenau. This dense oakland, the Sacred Grove of northern Alsace, was the haunt of hermits and in its core Arbogast had his cell. An oak tree of huge dimensions marks the spot. On the

Sketch (1803) showing the cloister ruins of the abbey of Niederhaslach after the French Revolution.

Niederhaslach. The Gothic church of St Florentius, formerly of the abbey.

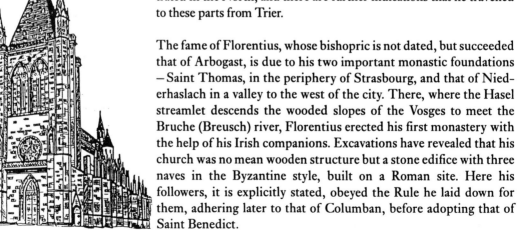

northern fringe of the forest Arbogast's first monastery was founded — Surburg, destroyed in the Thirty Years' War. The abbey church has since been restored to house the founder's tomb. His effigy is also in an old Gothic sanctuary in the centre of Surburg village. The cult of Arbogast was widely spread throughout Alsace, but his ministry was concentrated in the North, and there are further indications that he travelled to these parts from Trier.

The fame of Florentius, whose bishopric is not dated, but succeeded that of Arbogast, is due to his two important monastic foundations — Saint Thomas, in the periphery of Strasbourg, and that of Niederhaslach in a valley to the west of the city. There, where the Hasel streamlet descends the wooded slopes of the Vosges to meet the Bruche (Breusch) river, Florentius erected his first monastery with the help of his Irish companions. Excavations have revealed that his church was no mean wooden structure but a stone edifice with three naves in the Byzantine style, built on a Roman site. Here his followers, it is explicitly stated, obeyed the Rule he laid down for them, adhering later to that of Columban, before adopting that of Saint Benedict.

102

Louis the Pious, son of Charlemagne, caused a new church to be built over the Haslach foundation to receive the remains of the holy bishop Florentius who was first buried in Saint Thomas in Strasbourg, where he died. The *translatio* took place on 7 November in the year 810 and was pronounced a feastday to be celebrated by the entire diocese, and so it has remained.

This is the *Florentiusfest*, held yearly on the Sunday following 7 November, when the shrine and a life-size wooden statue of the patron saint are borne in procession around the village of Niederhaslach. Later in the day pilgrims visit Oberhaslach, where they pray in the Chapelle Saint-Florent. Haslach, whether *Ober* (Upper) or *Nieder* (Lower), are modest enough villages to harbour so majestic a church, but once the bishops of Strasbourg had their summer residence here and the place was not divided. Endless disasters befell the peaceful valley resort, religious wars, peasant revolts and repeated incursions of warring nations breaching the town's fortifications. Haslach, its abbey and episcopal palace burnt to the ground in the Thirty Years' War, only recovered in the form of two straggling villages, the lower of which rallies round the church – all that is left of the great abbey, sacked by the Swedes. This is the edifice we find today, the third, built in 1385 under the auspices of Augustinian canons, under whose rule Haslach enjoyed a period of rare peace and prosperity, evident in its proud structure. The west façade with its slender Gothic portal bearing the legend of Saint Florentius carved on its tympanum is the work of a son of Erwin von Steinbach, the builder of Strasbourg's fabulous cathedral. He is buried inside the church, having fallen to his death from a scaffold during its erection. Near his tomb we encounter again the story of Florentius, as a worker of miracles, in one of the stained-glass windows for which Niederhaslach is famed (the fourth window to the right: plate 10). The altar of Saint Brigid is gone, but Florentius' relics are in a niche in the choir, his gilded shrine of 1716 replacing a priceless reliquary that was robbed in 1525, when the saints remains were scattered on the church floor. Taken to safety, restored to the church, then hidden again in various private houses, they were eventually brought here to rest after the French Revolution.

Apart from these persecutions, Saint Florentius' remains were for centuries the object of fierce controversy, both Strasbourg and

Shrine of St Florentius in the church choir, Niederhaslach.

103

Haslach claiming to possess them and pursuing what was called 'The War of the Relics'.

The emperor Karl IV was obliged to intervene personally in 1353 and examine the contents of two reliquaries. To the joy of the Augustinian friars he confirmed that the saint's remains were indeed in Haslach. Gratified, they presented the monarch with an arm of their holy patron, that he took with him to his residence in Prague. A special altar was provided for the relic in the cathedral, and there it has remained.

Florentius had started off with a hermitage in the wooded Hasel valley, near what is now Oberhaslach. Several place-names in the vicinity bear out the tradition of this eremitic community, to the northeast of the village. Such 'priests' quarters' find reference in Strasbourg's early diocesan files as *Zu den Schotten*, or *de Scoti*, of the Irish – a place wiped away by the wars.

Western façade of the church of Marmoutier (Maursmünster).

If the pilgrim's resort of Oberhaslach was kept alive by oral tradition the old Roman road takes us on from there in northeasterly direction to Marlenheim, a seat of Merovingian kings. It is they who granted Florentius land, the proximity of which reminds one of the miracle of the healing of king Dagobert's daughter, portrayed in stone and painted glass in Niederhaslach's Gothic church. In Meren-heim's royal palace our hermit saint on arrival must have hung up his cloak on the sunbeam, as recorded!

Part of the King's Road, the *regia strata* between Strasbourg and Metz in Lorraine, has been identified. It led from Strasbourg to Itten-heim, where Saint Brigid had her sanctuary, and passed Merlenheim to make a stop at the 'Three Taverns', *Tres Tabernae*, now Saverne (Zabern), before crossing the river Zorn into Lorraine. Saverne, patron-ized by Romans and Celts before the Franks, had a church affiliated to the abbey of Maursmünster, that lies on this historic route and should not be missed by even the most hurried of visitors – in French Marmoutier.

It is not hard to be impressed by the nobility of the west façade of Maursmünster, representing, in the red sandstone of the region, Romanesque architecture at its purest. In northern Alsace it certainly takes the prize. It is called after the fourth abbot of the monastic settlement of Leobardus, said to be one of the original twelve Irish

104

companions of Columban, and the first to depart from Luxeuil on a mission. Leobardus is perhaps identical with Liuberat, the founder-abbot of the island monastery of Reichenau. Here in Alsace he was granted the large, primeval territory of Aquilea near Marlenheim, chosen residence of Austrasian kings, and the grant was enacted by Childebert II, who died in 595. Part of the *Cella Leobardi* has been discovered under the church aisle and can be visited together with the cryptal chamber of Leobardus, which is under the choir.

After the conflagration of the 8th century, Maur rebuilt the abbey and reformed the Rule and its earlier history passed into oblivion. As so often the case when Benedictines took over from their Columban predecessors, our information is extremely scant. We know little more about the 6th century inception of this abbey, to reach the peak of its fame in the 12th century, than that it was dedicated to the saints Peter, Paul and Martin. The demise of Leobardus is given as 618.

St Erhard. Statue in Ulm cathedral, Bavaria.

Who is this Er(h)ard we come across in so many churches, at so many altars, often as the guardian of hospitals, yet seldom with a church of his own like that mentioned in Strasbourg?

A forerunner of Boniface in the work of organization in Bavaria Erhard (Herardus) – Iorard? – was an assiduous church politician, whose mission took him in the 7th century to lands where Germanic tribes were endeavouring to settle down. His activity, prompted by local rulers, was not propitious for creating an image endearing Erhard to the people at large, who, however, sought his intercession as a healer, especially in posthumous water cures. But even if he is more respected than loved, Erhard's place is as secure in folklore as it is in hagiography which, apart from reference to him in calendars and liturgies, has several biographies to show, written down from the 11th century on. Alas, the lateness of these *vitae* calls for caution. Confusing comments in them gave rise to scholarly discussions, some of them leading to the opinion that we should strip *Sanctus Herardus Scotus* of his Irish identity entirely – an identity taken for granted through the ages, with a variety of documents describing the saintly bishop as *genere Scoticus, natione scotus, in Scotia natus, in vetere Scotia* etc., etc.

We might refer the hypersceptical to earlier traditions in Alsace, concerning the deposit of relics of Saint Brigid in Strasbourg by

Niedermünster. The abbey ruins, today.

105

Erhard, to be considered along with those familiar traits of an *episcopus vagans* which he displayed. Indeed, the mobility of Erhard was so inimitably Irish, that he probably belongs to those bishops discredited by Boniface because of their wandering habits. For it is odd that such a meritorious 7th-century church leader only found recognition in Rome in the 11th century, when he was canonized by an Alsatian pope. This pontiff, Leo IX, was of the progeny of Etichon and naturally well aware of the many Vosges churches founded by Erhard, and he ordered the reconstruction of a Merovingian monastery destroyed by the Hungarians, to which Erhard was intimately connected in legend: the convent of Saint Odilia on the foothills of the Vosges.

This little introduction to Saint Erhard leads us up the Mont-Sainte-Odile, called the Holy Mountain of Alsace 'where all roads meet', drawing, as it does, pilgrims and tourists alike to the tomb of this daughter of Eticho and the patron saint of his duchy.

Epitaph and design in relief on the sarcophagus of St Odilia, Mont-Saint-Odile.

Erhard christened the fifteen-year-old Odilia, born blind, upon which eyesight was miraculously bestowed on her. This occurred in Burgundy, in the convent of Palma (now Baume-les-Dames on the river Doubs) that observed the Columban Rule. It was there that Odilia had found refuge after repulsion by her pagan father because of her debility. Later repentant, the duke ceded his summer residence Hohenburg on Mount Altitona for a monastic settlement at his daughter's wish. And here Odilia presided as abbess, succouring the poor and preaching to the people, until her death around the year 720.

Such is the foundation story, elaborated on by generations of pilgrims taking the steep climb to Odilia's sanctuary and bathing their eyes in the holy well at the foot of the mount, where in 707 Odilia, encouraged by Erhard, built a subordinate convent with hospice attached to provide for supplicants unable to make the ascent. This grew into the great abbey of legend, Niedermünster, or Niederhohenburg, donated and enriched by Charlemagne and later kings and emperors who stopped there. Its basilica, in ruins, can be found near the well in the forest clearing.

As expressly stated in Odilia's *vita*, she 'eagerly welcomed the Irish' to her monasteries. This can be attributed to the asylum granted her in Palma and also to her indebtedness to Erhard.

When wandering through the convent buildings on what is now

106

Mont-Sainte-Odile, last enlarged by the emperor Frederick I Barbarossa in the 12th century, we follow the east wing, which is the oldest tract and pass through the Holy Cross chapel containing Eticho's stone coffin, into Odilia's sepulchral chamber. Here, where she breathed her last, a chapel was installed in the 8th century. The saint's sepulchre is adorned with a stone relief showing the christening of Odilia by Erhard, who is described in the inscription beneath as: *Beatus vir Herardus Ratisponensis episcopus . . .* In 'Ratispona' (the city of Regensburg in Bavaria) we will meet this great prelate again.

After passing through Augustinian and Benedictine hands, it is today the turn of Franciscan nuns to cater for guests at Mont-Sainte-Odile. Visitors who succumb to the magic of the place find lodging in the convent of Alsace's patron saint (plate 24).

In a beautiful lake setting of the southern Vosges there is a popular French holiday resort called Gérardmer. It has also intriguing legends to offer in the wide expanse of its forests. One concerns Charlemagne on a royal hunt, another, Columban in flight; reminders of the period anterior to 1576 when the whole region was divided between the duke of Lorraine and the chapter of the Columban convent of Remiremont. 'La Roche Saint-Colomban', a granite boulder which was said to have split apart to give the saint refuge while his pursuers rushed by, can be seen on a well-marked walk around the forest lakes beside the Pont des Fées, a bridge that has straddled the Volgone rivulet since medieval times.

The mountain pass leading from Gérardmer to Colmar in Alsace touches many places with Irish associations, such as in the valleys of the Münster and the Lauch, where the interesting church of Lautenbach greets us — not a Columban, but a Honau foundation dated 730. This fact is confirmed by the patronage of Saint Michael, whose baroque image adorns what is left of the 11th-century Augustinian abbey with its curious carvings. We take note also of Saint Wendalin in a striking pose among his farm animals — a coloured wooden relief of around the year 1500 (side altar).

In the vicinity of Lautenbach, tucked away in another green valley we come upon the remains of the great Benedictine abbey of

Murbach — the east end of its church, in spite of amputation, still monumental. Murbach is believed to have sprung from a settlement of Irish hermits, who had an altar to Saint Gall here when Pirmin arrived in 727 to take it over. Pirmin, himself a 'wandering bishop' of undefined 'Celtic' identity, had recently been expelled from the island monastery of Reichenau.

In Murbach we are in reach of the famous Alsatian wine route, bordering the Rhine. There we should look out for Rouffach, a small town where, on the gentle slope of its vineyards, large letters proclaim: CLOS ST LANDELIN.

The choicest of Alsatian wines are produced here in Rouffach, and stopping to savour them we honour both saint and proprietor — proud to greet a guest from Landelin's homeland. Studying his wine-card we read in French: 'Saint Landelin, an Irish prince, came to preach the Gospel. Around the year 640 he suffered the death of martyrdom. In the 8th century the bishop of Strasbourg donated to the 'Monks of Landelin' stocks cultivated on the best wine-growing slopes of Alsace, since titled "Saint Landelin's Vineyard".'

Old ex libris woodcut, depicting the martyrdom of St Landelin. Used by the Rouffach vineyard as a logo.

A leap over the Rhine again into the Ortenau (Breisgau) will take the curious to the haunts of this Landelin (Landolino; in the oldest form Lendlin), a trip taken since time immemorial by the inhabitants of Rufach (Rouffach) and other Alsatian parishes to Ettenheimmünster. There they take part in a long procession, headed with a silver bust reliquary carried on a bier, and an old *Landelinus-Litanei* is sung while they trace the grounds of the abbatial domain, long since disappeared. Riders also make the round, carrying a banner and a relic of the saint, and their horses are blessed on the green beside the holy well. A beautiful and imposing church adjoins the well's sanctuary — Saint Landelin's. Built in 1688 and enlarged again in the 18th century to serve the never abating concourse of visitors, it superseded former pilgrim churches on the spot where the saint was martyred. The new altar, erected by the abbot of Ettenheimmünster in 1688, carried an inscription in golden letters — *S Landelinus Scotiae Regis Filius*, followed by a Latin hymn of praise with an explicative second verse:

108

Quinque fontes semper manant	Five sources always flowing
Landelini meritis,	are Landelin's merit,
Aegros, caecos, claudos sanant,	healing the sick, blind and lame,
Sors magna est inclytis.	famed among nobility.

Today the high altar of Saint Landelin's has an oil painting of the 'glorification' of its patron, while a side-altar shows him in a wooden statue as a young man. Only in the baroque period did this image appear; older ones portray Landelin as a mature, bearded man, often crowned, in princely robes. On the ceiling the legend is told in seventeen frescos, the first two of which — starting to the right of the west entrance, show the saint's departure from Ireland.

It seems that the cult of Saint Landelin set in straight after his death at the hands of a local huntsman, infuriated by the conduct of his hounds, who refused to chase deer in the vicinity but became meek and docile when nearing the hermit's cell. The huntsman had the backing of his pagan lord, Gisico, who considered Landelin a sorceror.

Pilgrim church of St Landelin, Ettenheimmünster, with dome over the holy well. (Lithograph of 1880.)

There in the glade, where Landelin lay outstretched in his blood, spring water gushed forth from under the severed head and at each limb's extremity. The five sources (some legends say there were four) soon formed a basin, to which the natives resorted, and bathing, found healing there for many ills. Anchorites, settling in the neighbourhood, were gathered together in the early 8th century by the bishop of Strasbourg to form a colony and provide for an increasing number of pilgrims to the spot. Out of this first *cella monachorum* grew, with time, the impressive resort we find there now.

It was Etto (Eddo), the succeeding bishop of Strasbourg in the 8th century, who caused another monastery to be erected a little further up the valley for thirty Benedictines. Etto was deeply impressed by the miracles at the well, over which he had a new sanctuary built. His interest may reflect Irish sympathies, for, before becoming bishop of Strasbourg, he was abbot of Reichenau, in direct succession to Pirmin.

Baroque interior of the church of St Landelin, Ettenheim-münster.

Etto's monastery, built in honour of Landelin, was given the name of its founder — *Monachium divi Ettonis* — to become 'Ettenheim-Münster'. Incorporating the pilgrim church of Saint Landelin's, it cherished the saint's memory through more than a thousand troubled years.

Nothing remains but a monastery wall of this once great seat of learning, a centre of theology and music, radiating into the Rhine valley and influencing its spiritual and cultural life for centuries. The percussions caused by the French Revolution and the Seculari-zation of 1803 saw its library scattered, its archives in ashes, its monks finally dispersed and the huge complex razed to the ground after having served as a factory. This all has left us with a great void, not only concerning Ettenheimmünster's early history but also that of its Irish patron saint.

Of the few items salvaged from the abbey after confiscation in 1803 the most precious was the bust-reliquary of Saint Landelin, made in 1506 as a recipient for the saint's skull. It was taken to the pilgrim church of Saint Landelin, acting from then on as the parish church, and is kept in the sacristy, to be exposed on special occasions. That it was saved goes to the credit of an undaunted parish priest, pouring condemnation on the heads of those involved in transport-ing the bust on a cart to the smelting foundry. To eschew the fires of hell they unloaded it, dropping it into a ditch.

The reliquary, a prime work of art of the late Gothic period, portrays the bust of Saint Landelin in chased silver (plate 4). Bejew-elled and embossed, it contains the saint's skull, and has, inserted on the chest, a figuration of the martyrdom, whereby circles around the outstretched limbs and severed head demonstrate the pools of rising water. Scenes from the life of the saint surround the base of the reliquary, and these are especially interesting, for they follow early legends that were recorded from oral tradition. Here the true *peregrinus* confronts us, with satchel and staff. This is what we are told:

Crossing the Rhine, into the wilds of the Alemanni, Landelin makes his first stop at the house of a certain Edulf, where the village of Altdorf now stands, at the foot of the northern Black Forest range. Here he wanders off up the valley of the Undiz to where it is joined by the Luttenbach, a little stream — today Lautenbach — and builds himself a hut in the forest glade. Animals befriend him, especially deer, who bring him food.

Full of misgivings, Edulf's wife and three daughters set out from

110

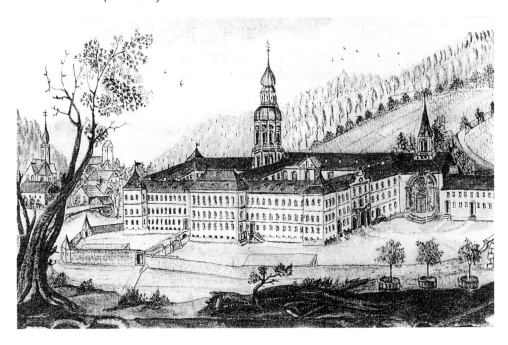

Altdorf to search for Landelin, accompanied by a guide. One of the daughters is blind, and when they come across the body of the murdered hermit, she is left behind there, while the others go for help. She touches her eyes with fingers stained from Landelin's blood, and is cured from her blindness. Returning with the intention of bringing their friend's corpse back and over the Rhine to receive a Christianburial, which could not be afforded on the right side of the river, Edulf's family are convinced by the miracle of the hermit's sanctity. They carry his remains down the valley, to a place where, having put the load down for a rest, they find it impossible to raise it again. Even a team of oxen brought there with a cart, cannot move the corpse. This, it is decided, is a sign from heaven that Landelin wished to be buried there, and that they proceed to do. They stick the hermit's staff into the grave to mark the spot, and it sprouts green leaves. This eventually grows into a huge oak tree. The church that was built there, where first anchorites had their hermitage, is the Münchweier parish church of today, where under the mensa of the altar the tomb with Landelin's relics are kept. The centre of the

18th-century watercolour of the abbey of Ettenheimmünster shortly before demolition. On left, St Landelin's church with Münchweier beyond.

111

cult, however, has always been the site of his martyrdom and the sanctuary with the holy sources.

Since Landelin's Irish origin is today questioned for no other reason than that his name 'sounds Frankish', it would be gratifying to find in the geneologies of Ireland a (F)lann, born around 600, who went abroad on a pilgrimage.

A young rider heads the procession with a relic of St Landelin around Ettenheim-münster's former abbey demesne.

Bordering the Rhine in the southern Black Forest the patron saint of the beautiful Münstertal valley is faced with similar mistrust. This is Trudpert, by all medieval accounts and hailed in oral tradition as an Irish apostle.

Trudpert's footsteps, like those of Landolin, appear to lead from Alsace. His benefactor is Otpert, a lord of the famed Habsburg dynasty, then situated on the left bank of the Rhine. Otpert encounters Trudpert, an Irish pilgrim returning from Rome in 604, and — prompted by political motives, no doubt — gives him two workmen to assist in the erection of a monastic settlement on the far side of the Rhine. Trudpert's mission in Breisgau is of short duration, however, for after only three years of labour he is murdered by the workmen beside his hermitage in Münstertal, some say for attempting to build a church in nearby Krozingen.

Trudpert's *monasterium* was considered the first of its kind to be installed on the east bank of the Rhine. In 643, Otpert had the martyr's remains ceremoniously disinterred and enshrined, which amounted to a canonization. The day of the *translatio*, 26 April, is celebrated as the saint's feastday. Another tradition reflecting his origin is that he was a brother of Saint Rupert, a view following the ancient belief that this patron saint of Salzburg was also an Irishman. More trustworthy is the Columban connexion hinted at — brethren from Luxeuil having first laboured with Trudpert in Alsace, before the fateful step was taken by him to attempt to convert the Alemanni beyond the Rhine. Be that as it may, a certainty is that Trudpert's foundation half-way up the Black Forest valley continued to exist down to its secularization in 1807, twelve hundred years after the saint's demise.

Trudpert's foundation was an *Eigenkirche* with inherent seignorial rights attached, and it remained in the donor's family for many

generations. We learn of restorations carried out by a descendant of
Otpert in the year 815, concerning perhaps the *Oratorium*, as mentioned in 860, and three 10th-century renovations are also recorded,
showing the house of Habsburg's vested interest in the monastery
that preceded the proud Benedictine abbey complex we encounter
today. Although unable to avoid entirely the blows of its persecutors,
Sankt Trudpert still presents one of the most prodigious monastic
edificies in southwest Germany.

Enrichened by its neighbouring silver-mines, the abbey was a
great prey and harried and plundered incessantly. After destruction
in the Thirty Years' War it rose from its ashes to even more splendour. Peter Thumb, who built the famous abbey library of Sankt
Gallen, made the design and Italian artists were brought in to embellish
it. Thus the inhabitants of the valley were aptly rewarded for the
untiring attachment shown towards their old Irish apostle. This
veneration found expression in a great store of lore, documented in
baroque illustrations in the new abbey church. Now that of the
parish, it shows over the high altar Trudpert beside a forest tree
holding the axe that slew him, his hermitage in the background. An
altar to the right in an exquisite marble framework depicts the saint
ascending, in the valley beneath the great abbey in its prime.

*Münstertal valley with St
Trudpert's monastery. Chapel
and well to the left.*

Over the church nave a cycle of ceiling paintings portray the
patron's life story in eight scenes, beginning with his departure from
Ireland, opposite the north entrance and continuing clockwise. To
the left of the high altar in the choir lie buried the Habsburg duke
and his descendants, seven of whom are named in an epitaph
honouring their noble donations.

An avenue of old lime trees shades the pathway up an incline to
the abbey. Devoid of its Benedictine monks it now accommodates a
convent for the nuns of Saint Joseph and a home for the aged.

A little to the east of the church stands the chapel of Saint
Trudpert, built above the saint's well. Steps lead down to the oratory
with the holy well, frequented still by those seeking a cure, and
pilgrims, responsible for the lighted candles and flowers left on the
white, cradle-like cenotaph in the centre.

The chapel above was built in 1697. Cruciform, it replaces an
earlier round one, the iconography of which it happily took over.

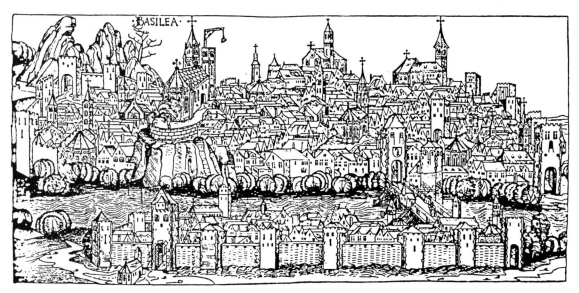

Basel in 1493. The woodcut from Schedel's World Chronicle shows the minster rebuilt on its mound, with one tower unfinished.

Irish propensity to monasticism seems to be reflected in effigies of Saint Augustin and Pope Gregory the Great, who flank Trudpert, pictured with his axe, in nobleman's dress. Also depicted are the assassins, fleeing from the building under construction, while Otpert rushes to the scene. Side altars in the chapel portray saints that were always considered to be Irish – Fridolin and Rupert, the latter with his sister Ehrentrud, both of Salzburg. On one of the doors leading behind the main altar we find Trudpert painted again, in the company of these two supposed relatives visiting Rome, while on the opposite door is shown his historic meeting with Otpert in Alsace, on returning from Rome (plate 2).

This chapel with the well is the centre of Trudpert's cult. Yearly on his feastday colourful processions in Black Forest dress turn up with bands of musicians to celebrate their patron. An early 18th-century reliquary is then borne around the precincts of the former monastery in what is called the 'Trudperti-Umgang' (plate 19).

Was Trudpert Irish, as Black Forest tradition insists, or simply an inmate of the great Irish missionary centre in Luxeuil? We will never know. But the impact he made is that of an Irish *peregrinus* and his posthumous fame was undoubtably well deserved. That alone is enough for Ireland to be proud of.

114

THE UPPER RHINE
(HOCHRHEIN)

Beyond the sharp turn that the Rhine (Hochrhein) takes at Basel to face the North, imprints of Columban become clearer, his cult gains ground. On his arrival, Basel's episcopal seat of Roman times had crumbled, and that of Ragnachar of Luxeuil was yet to take over. A pupil of Columban's successor Eustasius, Ragnachar brought, no doubt, the cults of Luxeuil to the bishopric of Augst-Basel, in process of restoration. Soon, the extending sovereignity of the Etichon dynasty was to reach Basel, linking it to the Strasbourg episcopate – a measure not likely to change its disposition.

In medieval times, Columban's feastday was held regularly in the cathedral of Basel, the one we visit today, where Fridolin also had his altar. The famous sculptured portal of 1200, the *Galluspforte* leading into Saint Gall's chapel in the minster, still answers to the name of that most distinguished of Columban's companions. Inside, spoliation has obliterated many Irish associations, although Irish apostles stood high in the favour of Emperor Heinrich II, canonized soon after his death for his own missionary exploits. Saint Henry attended the inauguration of Basel's new cathedral in 1019. A similar partiality is noted in the cathedral the emperor inaugurated in the Franconian town of Bamberg in 1012, where Irish saints are revered.

In the environs of Basel, there are many dedications to early Irish missionaries. In Blotzheim, northwest of the city, Columban has his

Design on the modern bronze door of St Fridolin's church, Stetten.

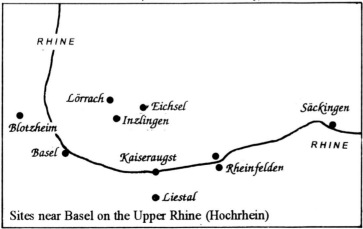

Sites near Basel on the Upper Rhine (Hochrhein)

Säckingen, from the Swiss side of the Rhine. St Fridolin's minster and the Gallus tower, right — once on an island.

fountain, and across the Rhine in Lörrach devotion to Fridolin claims our attention.

Who would guess, that in the municipality of Lörrach, this congested area with an industrialized population, folk memory would not be choked to death? Yet Sankt Fridolin's, the parish church of Stetten, one of Lörrachs integrated communities, bears testimony to the stubborn abherence to ancient cults, and to their motivations. Stetten marks a stop made by Fridolin, travelling from Austrasia and over the Rhine in pursuit of his lonely ambition in the 6th century.

A boulder, shaped like a pulpit and called the *Fridolinsfels*, stood ever since like a road-block on the old forest path between Stetten and Inzlingen. It was here that, according to tradition, Fridolin preached to the people, using the towering rock as would a public orater. And thus it remained, the tidings of this strange pilgrim having made an indelible impression on his surroundings. It needed the profanity of the epoch we live in to remove by force, in the name of boundary reforms, the boulder from its hallowed place.

Inzlingen, with its moated castle, is a stone's throw away from Eichsel. Now part of Rheinfelden, with its port that signals the end of major shipping on the Rhine, Eichsel's church is dedicated to Saint Gall. The same applies to Kaiseraugst across the river, once a Roman *castrum* and bridgehead. Kaiseraugst's church of Sankt Gallus has Gothic mural paintings depicting scenes from the life of the apostle. As so often the case with Saint Gall, a patronage of Saint Brigid is near at hand where he passed by. Proud to claim parentage with *Naomh Bríghid*, it is likely that he himself deposited relics taken from Kildare along the route. This would apply to Liestal, an important stop on a trade passage of antiquity. In the parochial archives of Liestal, a town a little south of Kaiseraugst, appears a church of 'Sankt Prigithae' possessing a relic of its patron saint, still on record in the year 1608.

It may be here, about 10 kilometres from Basel, beyond the river bend, that Columban's party decided to leave the course of the Rhine they had followed so long and so diligently upstream from Koblenz. They forsook the guidance of the waterway, hampered now by the youthful exuberance of the Upper Rhine, and faced the Alps, where we shall hear of their adventures in due course. If the direction was changed at Liestal, they could proceed to find the Limmat tributary and the lake of Zürich.

116

It is quite likely, however, that the little troop went on, either to branch off the Rhine at the mouth of the Aare river, or else to take a short cut up to the Limmat at an old Roman bridgehead at Laufenburg, that provided communications with the South. Laufenburg came in medieval times into the possession of the important royal abbey of Sankt Fridolin in Säckingen. On our passage upstream from Basel, between these two bridgeheads on the Rhine it is Säckingen we encounter.

This is a neat little town with therapeutic baths, seated on the right bank of the Upper Rhine. Backed by the slopes of the Black Forest, it faces the Swiss Jura, and is dominated by a large Gothic edifice in baroque attire – Saint Fridolin's Minster. Its appearance is consistent with its historic past, being the successor of an abbey church in Crown possession that dominated the region. Beneath it, the town of Säckingen grew up to acquire a sedate, residential look, such as may be expected from a society governed by abbesses and canonesses of nobility, exercising their judicial authority since the year 878. This is the date given for the abbey donation to Saint Richgardis, wife of Karl III of Alemannia, a weak Carolingian king, later nominated *Kaiser*. Richgard held sway over an institution with far-reaching domains on both sides of the Rhine. She was succeeded by other abbesses of royal blood, who solidated the monastery's position as an instrument of political weight, with influence on state affairs throughout the Middle Ages. It was able to retain independant status down to the Secularization of 1806 – the last chapter of an eventful history that is our concern insofar as Säckingen evolves from the Merovingian decree accorded to Fridolin. He is the initiator and patron saint of a great abbey that has always upheld its Irish heritage.

For it was here that Fridolin, soon after the year 500, finally reached the goal of his desires. Discovering a water-bound refuge between two arms of the Rhine, he recognized the island of his dreams and proceeded to fulfill his pledge to the memory of Saint Hilarius by setting up a missionary station on it for the conversion of the Alemannic population.

This undertaking was not as easy as it sounds. Although armed with Clovis' grant, the idea did not appeal to the locals, a tribe using the Rhine island with its broken-down Celto-Roman remains for cattle-grazing. Ignoring the authority of the king of the Franks, they turned Fridolin out, and he had difficulty getting back. It needed a visit to the

The legend of the foundation of Säckingen,
shown on plaques of the Gothic period,
in the church treasury.

a) *Fridolin's dream.*

b) *Fridolin dams the Rhine.*

c) *He raises Urso to life.*

d) *He causes Urso to give testimony at court.*

e) *Fridolin and the skeleton.*

118

bishop of Chur in far-away Rhaetia and the support of the Alpine lord, Urso of Glarus, to enable Fridolin to realize his ambition. Urso decreed that Fridolin would inherit the island after his death, but the will was contested by Urso's brother. The story of Fridolin resurrecting Urso from his grave in order to give testimony in court in his favour is quite the most popular motive in the saint's iconography. At every turn, within or without Saint Fridolin's Minster, on its façade, in the vestibule, on the church ceiling, on the shrine, in stone effigies and altar pieces, we are confronted with Fridolin leading a skeleton by the hand.

Procession with the golden shrine through the streets of Säckingen on St Fridolin's feastday

Fridolin got his island at length. He threw tree trunks into the stream to prevent the cattle crossing, and built first a chapel to Saint Hilarius, then conceiving a monastery on the lines of Kildare. Of this, after the Hungarian onslaught of 917, only the nunnery arose again. This proved nevertheless to be of great durability.

Fridolin, in his lifetime, performed many engineering feats, long remembered. He drained the island in an admirable manner, and set about changing the river's course in order to attach the island to the northern mainland – as we find it today. Indeed, his meritorious performance has gained Fridolin the patronage of hydraulic structures and those who work them (plate 1).

Fridolin died in Säckingen in 538 or 540. His sepulchre under the choir of the present church is now empty, but his relics are displayed in a magnificent shrine of solid silver, commissioned by the last abbess before the convent's final suppression. This masterpiece of rococo art, shaped in the form of a state coach, is in Saint Fridolin's chapel, to the right of the high altar, protected from theft by a double grating. On 6 March, the saint's feastday, it is carried through the town in great pomp. In the flagged streets the colours of Ireland are not lacking, nor, in the procession, is the Irish ambassador to Germany.

The veneration of Fridolin, shown to be deeply rooted and widespread, must have begun soon after his death. The cult, with rural accents, reached out far into the Alpine valleys of Switzerland, with the canton of Glarus claiming Fridolin as its patron and converter, and carrying his image in its coat of arms. In Säckingen alone, the size of the crypt – a commodious, round structure of the 9th-century Carolingian period – points to the crowds of pilgrims seeking access to the saint's tomb. This, together with Fridolin's mention in a 9th-century liturgical manuscript from Zürich, gives us an inkling of what early abbey documents, lost in the fire of 1272, would have contained.

St Fridolin guards the new tollbridge over the Rhine; the minster and the Black Forest in the background.

Time and again reduced to rubble, by war and strife, the abbey always managed to rise again. Now an 18th-century church narrates to us the story of Fridolin in its sumptuous, ornate interior. A series of frescos fill the ceiling, giving us the legend concerning Säckingen and its inception. A large oil painting by an Italian artist crowns the high altar, portraying Fridolin together with Hilarius, his precursor and ideal in far-off Poitiers, who – how could it be otherwise? – is the church's minor patron.

The church treasury, behind Saint Fridolin's altar, guards what is left of this rich and regal abbey. Perhaps the most intriguing item is the chasuble, said to be that of the saint, comprising a piece of embroidered cloth of 5th–6th-century Byzantine weaving.

A short walk along the Rhine promenade brings us past a Gallus fountain to the *Gallusturm*, a round tower that marks the tip of the former island. It was erected after a flood disaster in the Middle Ages to serve as part of a breakwater system. Saint Gall is also remembered in Säckingen's minster, where he seems to have always had his altar.

Like all early monasteries, the abbey had social functions to fulfill, and Irish pilgrims on their way to Rome made a regular stop here, where the municipality echoes its princely rank in a gracious layout of parks and gardens. The once palatial residence of Schönau today stores an interesting museum with Celtic, Roman, and early Christian objects. A little further downstream we come to a bridge spanning the Rhine, erected in 1976 to connect Germany with Switzerland. There again in the middle of the bridge he stands, facing his Island of Destiny, this Apostle of the Alemanni, not forgotten yet; the most extraordinary of all those intrepid pioneers who took it upon themselves to carry the cross of a *peregrinatio pro Christo* eastward.

From prehistoric times down to those of the early Christians, settlers were attracted to the banks of this section of the Rhine, that carved out a horizontal path for itself between the mountain ranges. Part of this preference was due to the nutritious food, supplied in overabundance in the form of fish – salmon coming up as far as the Falls of Schaffhausen to spawn. The 19th century with its power stations put an end to the *wanderlust* of the salmon – that of our Irish monks and pilgrims having long since subsided. Characteristic of the Hochrhein are the tortuous

120

twists and bends forced on the river before it can settle down on its westward flow. There, just beyond the Schaffhausen Falls, where water erosion dug deepest to form a channel, man, quick to take the advantages nature offers for his survival, made use of the available tongues of land between the curves for habitation. Here the Romans, in their Alpine campaign of the year 15 BC, were confronted with a formidable *murus Gallicus*. They overcame the barricade and destroyed the peninsular *oppidum* of the Celts.

In their turn, Germanic tribes bore down from the North and reached the river boundary. Soon these settlers were themselves subjected to harassment, but of a doctrinal nature. Small bands of Irish monks were working their way upstream.

We know little about the eremitic community that first settled on this peninsula of the Rhine, since called the Island of Rheinau. They are first noted in 778, but can be dated earlier. Awed by the jutting rocks in the stupendous cataract of Schaffhausen, river barges and rafts unloaded there and, after portage, wares were reloaded. This process led to the establishment of a depot, and a marketing place for tradesmen grew up on the southern bank.

The bridge on to the island of Rheinau, with its abbey church.

In 858, King Ludwig der Deutsche, engaged in consolidating his Franconian heritage, recognized the political and cultural importance of the little monastic establishment near the site. He strengthened the position of the monks of Rheinau and, putting them under obligations, accredited them with autonomous status and granted them immunity. The way was paved for the flourishing Benedictine abbey that was to follow.

The Rheinau monastery – in textual reference sometimes referred to as *Augia minor* in contradistinction to Reichenau, *Augia major* – first gained renown through its Irish patron Saint Findan who, after imposing his own monastic rule on the community, died there after years of severe ascetic confinement. Belonging to the 9th century, Findan is not our concern here, but his *Vita*, written by a contemporary, is of great historical value. It preserves specimens of Old Irish, written on the Continent, that are the oldest we know of.

Those who are interested will find a stone effigy of Findan in Aazheimerhof, the summer residence of the abbots of Rheinau near Neuhausen at the Rhinefalls of Schaffhausen. On the island of Rheinau the patron's ornate marble sarcophagus also bears his image. It is in the

*Church choir, Rheinau.
Left, the sarcophagus of St
Findan, early 18th-century,
with statuette of the saint.*

choir of the baroque church, a great resort for pilgrims until Secularization. That the prestigious abbey had an altar dedicated to Saint Brigid recalls its long occupation by Irish monks and the veneration Saint Findan had for her. It was a cult certainly kept up by the Augustinians arriving here from Honau, who, as mentioned above, were thus compensated for the loss through flooding of their island monastery north of Strasbourg in the year 1290. They were given Rheinau, only to suffer the same fate again in a very short time.

If it is not possible for us to deal with every Rhine island the Irish *peregrini* set foot on, we still cannot leave this proudest of rivers without mention of the most renowned of them all – the Reichenau, situated at the outflow of the Bodensee (Lake Constance) that natives like to call the 'Suebian Sea'. This huge stretch of water the Alpine Rhine must traverse in search of a passage in which it can wind its way ultimately into the western ocean.

Pushing through the bottleneck of Konstanz into the outlet called the Untersee, the Rhine salutes to its right a flat island, bared of trees. This is the Reichenau. With a length of five kilometres, in width not exceeding one and a half, it was joined to the mainland in the 19th century with a dam. Over this we pass, a long ethereal avenue of poplars giving us the perfect approach to the monastic isle of fame, where, on reaching its banks, a modern statue of its patron saint Pirmin holds watch.

Who is Pirmin? His ethnicity worries hagiologists still. Like Findan of Rheinau, Pirmin's merits were of a reformative, less of an apostolic nature, his main achievement the deepening and consolidation of what had been sown before him in the field of Western Christendom. Under the wing of an emerging Carolingian dynasty, he was able to cover an immense range of missionary work. The Benedictines, who fostered his ideas, attributed foundations to Pirmin that were nevertheless beyond his scope. This can often simply signify that their saint's precepts came to be instituted in such places.

Pirmin's monastery is in Mittelzell, the centre of the island of Reichenau, and was probably founded in the year 724, decreed by Charles Martel, an ancester of Charlemagne. What remains is the minster, built for the royal abbey in 816. The nave of its lofty, impressive interior dates from that period.

We get a good idea of the benefactions attributed to Pirmin by the Benedictines who ruled the monastery throughout the ages, by viewing the large oil painting exhibited in the choir (plate 8). A model of ubiquity is presented, giving his blessing from a boat, the island and surrounding coastal districts sprinkled with spires of churches he instigated. In the centre Mittelzell appears as the huge monastic complex the 17th-century painter envisaged. As to the lake, he follows the traditon in depicting it to be alive with reptiles, snakes and sea-monsters fleeing the island haven – the extirpation of evil, portrayed in Pirmin's iconography, that he shares with Patricius; a feat of exorcism associated also with the apostles Martin and Hilarius and applied to sacred isles such as Lérins on the Mediterranean coast. Ancient symbolic gestures, they tell us nothing about Pirmin's origin.

Owing to his meritorious reputation, nations have been keen to claim Pirmin (Primenius). Suspected Mozarabic-Visigothic, Anglo-Saxon and other scribal traits were minutely examined. A Spanish, Aquitanian and Franconian background is suggested, as well as that of Ireland – the saint's homeland in local tradition. Pirmin is named in older texts as 'of Celtic stock', which makes an Irish claim plausible, supported as it is by the familiar description of him as a *peregrinus monachus* of habitual bishop-cum-abbot standing, opening up miraculous springs of water with his staff.

A protégé of the Franconian court Pirmin certainly was when he set off, armed with a deed. If we are to believe the records, he was dispatched to the lands of the Alemanni with instructions for stabilizing Christianity in that border colony and binding it firmly within the framework of the empire.

Pirmin, seen as a political envoy, reaped trouble and was pushed about between various places. But here on the island of Reichenau the cultural prestige of his monastery, fostered by the Benedictines, bore fruit.

Whether Irish or not, Pirmin and his *monachi peregrini* had on this island – as is elsewhere the case – Irish forerunners. Of the three early monastic churches on the Reichenau the first to greet us concerns just these: the former priory of Sankt Georg in Oberzell, that has barely changed in appearance since Carolingian days. Monastic traditions point to an even older foundation, the *cella Leobardi* of around 600, that recalls Columban's associate, the abbot Leobardus of Maursmünster,

Church of St George in Oberzell, island of Reichenau.

123

mentioned before. He has been identified with Liuberat, whose name heads the List of the Deceased in the Confraternity Book of Reichenau.

Despite its unassuming appearance, the church of Saint George reveals a rich interior, including a crypt (which had an altar dedicated to Saint Brigid) and three naves. Its mural paintings are celebrated, dating from the year 1000 at the latest, and of great artistic value. Discovered under the plaster of the 19th century these frescos are now sadly fading, having compared once undoubtedly in brilliance with the manuscript illuminations of the Middle Ages for which the Reichenau was famed.

Little wonder then, that the richly endowed island sanctuary was invariably raided. Its costly library, evacuated and dispersed for safety, was never to be retrieved again. But of the volumes since located, scholarly research has identified at least ten manuscripts, either complete or fragmentary, that belonged to the Reichenau scriptorium and can be ascribed to Ireland. Of these, the most remarkable is Adomnán's Life of Colmcille, the oldest transcription known to exist, written in Iona by the abbot Dorbbéne, who died in 713. The discovery was made by Father Stephan White in the 17th century. The codex is now in the municipal library of Schaffhausen.

The presence of such treasures on the Reichenau leads us to ponder on Pirmin's 'congregation of *peregrini*', as recalled by Rhabanus Maurus who died in 856 – a period when *peregrini* was a nomination synonymous with *Scoti*. Another chronicler recalled fifty books donated by them to the island monastery.

Pirmin himself is buried in Hornbach in the Palatinate, where he died in 753 after having crossed back over the Rhine.

INDEX